Mr. Boy

Tales of a Southern Gentleman

Ron Harris retired after a 40-year career as an educator, including 16 teaching Biology and Drama at Johnson High School and 20 years as director of Lee High's Drama Magnet Program. Ron received his B.S. in Biology from the University of Montevallo, and master's degrees from the University of Georgia (Biology) and University of Montevallo (Speech/Theatre). Ron received the 2000 Marion Gallaway Lifetime Achievement Award for Alabama Theatre, the 2006 Huntsville Volunteer of the Year Award, and the 2008 Virginia Hammill Simms Award. He has won numerous awards for his costume and set designs, and as a director his productions have been awarded state, regional and national high school theatre awards. Ron adapted his original play, *Like Moles, Like Rats*, for the screen, with the full-length film released under the title *Twenty Years After*. Ron is most proud of *Upon Their Shoulders: The Merrimack Story*, which he researched, wrote, directed and designed for his mentors Debra and Alan Jenkins of Merrimack Hall Performing Arts Center. He's lived in Huntsville, Alabama since 1971, but still calls Putnam, Alabama his home.

Mr. Boy

Tales of a Southern Gentleman

By

Ron Harris

D(C)G
Publications

First published in Greece 2011

DCG Publications
www.dcgmediagroup.com

ISBN 978-960-99470-4-6

Typeset by
DCG Publications

To my Mama and Daddy
For love and tolerance . . .
and freedom.

Thomas Ronald Harris

Acknowledgements

Emily Post said sending 'thank you' notes is the key to civilization. So Mr. Boy, constantly seeking civility, says 'thank you' to these believers: Teresa Connors, my muse; David Harwell, my manager; Mark Roberts, my starting gun; Dilcy Windham Hilley, my editor/best friend; Douglas Foote, my publisher; Kathryn Tucker Windham, my inspiration; Andrea McManus, typist/first wife"; Terry Jackson, spiritual spellchecker; Susanna Leberman, archivist; Michael Wood, electronic enabler; LeAnn Siefferman, artist; Ashley Dinges, closer; Debra and Alan Jenkins, head cheerleaders, and my sisters Celia Etheridge and Lena Carol Bishop, writing solitude/love/great food.

And these families, who at some time in my life fed me: Atkins, Beasley, Beck, BISHOP, Bombino, Burge, Butler, Carpenter, Carter, Compton, Countess, Cowert, Drake, Downey, ETHERIDGE, Flamberg, Gauldin, Gaut, Hall, Hamilton, HARRIS, Henderson, Hutchens, Johnson, Kirkpatrick, Little, Markow, Masterson, McClay, McGrew, McHugh, McManus, Overstreet, Padilino, Peck, Pike, Quillin, Robinson, Siegelman, Sharpe, Singleton, Sneed, Tetz, Twente, VanNetta, Vice, Vickers, Walters, Ward, West, Wilke, Windham, Yell, and Young.

And these friends: Aaron, Al, Allan, Amanda, Amy, Anita, Ashley, Azura, Barbara, Barry, Becky, Benny, Beth, Bette, Betty, Bil, Bill, Billy, Bob, Bonnie, Brenda, Brian, Bry, Cam, Carl, Charlie, Chris, Christie, Christina, Chuck, Class of 63, Claudia, Clay, Corey, Dan, Dana Lee, Daniel, David, Deborah, Delo, Denis, Denny, Diane, Dixie, Dorothy, Eugene, Facebook (734), Felicia, Fielding, Gary, Gaylen, Georgine, Gerald, Graham, Greg, Gregory, Hayley, Howard, Jackie, Jameel, James, Janet, Jerry, Jim, Jimmy, Joanna, Johnna, Joey, Jo Ellen, Jon, Jonathan, John,

i

Johnny, Josh, Joshua, Judy, Julia, Karl, Kathy, Kaye, Ken, Kenzie, Kevin, Kim, Lakin, Laura, Leah, Lee, Leland, Linda, Liz, Lucy, Lynn, Lynwood, Lysle, Margaret, Margaret Ann, Maria, Marie, Marshall, Mary Jane, Matt, Maxine, Melanie, Michael, Nathan, Nall, Neal, Pam, Pat, Paul, Penny, Randy, Ranee, Rebecca, Reg. E, Robbie, Robert, Ron, Sam, Sandon, Sandra, Sarah, Scott, Shannon, Shelby, Sheree, Sherri, Sherry, Skid, Sonja, Steve, Swiggie, Tamira, Teri, Tim, Tina, Titus, Tom, Tracey, Tricia, Tucker, Victor, Wade, Wilbert, and Wilson.

And for those friends that left early, before the party really got started: Kitti, Donna, Jerry, Ed, Eddie, Bobby, Steve, Buzzy, Sue, Jimmy, Bud, Mike, James, Robby, Greg, Lee, David, Crump, Jason, Junior, and Fred.

Introduction

"Go home and tell stories. Share them. Write them. The best stories begin at home." Kathryn Tucker Windham, Alabama's storyteller laureate, ends her story-telling events with this mantra. She has just taken you on a timeless journey to her place of joy that always resonates with your past, with a flash of something lost suddenly cutting the crowded air, clearing the gray of half remembrance, and then water-coloring it into the blue of lost October skies. Coupled with that may be a singular smell, or a cool wind that causes your arms to hold yourself a little bit tighter, because she has graciously given you a free ticket to ride into the past... and that ticket is already punched.

Mrs Windham told me to write what I knew. I always thought it was too little, too personal. She said it didn't matter... just tell it. If it's big enough for you, it's big enough, she seemed to say.

And so I write these remembrances, not editing myself as my California muse, Teresa Conners, instructs me in so many precise words. This hodgpogeny of stories is a conversation with myself. It's a pleasure to have you in the room listening.

I had an hermetically sealed youth on a dirt road in Southwest Alabama that cut through a land grant of 40 acres bequeathed by a relative circa 1835. Its horizon was the moon and its mornings were slices of light topping loblolly pines with new days holding adventure. My parents, Helen and Willard Harris, let me open gates in pastures not plowed or planted. They let me eat whatever landed in my hands as I stretched them to the sky.

You can have some of this manna. I was always blessed with

just a little bit more than I needed. My "eyes were bigger than my stomach," my Mama would scold, or my Daddy would say, "No one needs a third piece of pie."

Here's my Mama's lemon ice box pie with tiny golden beads of sugar on the meringue, shining like baby suns.

You can have the last piece; I don't need it. I'm full.

August 10, 2010

Mama & Daddy

Table of Contents

My Mama: Miss Helen

Daddy was probably unclogging the outside grease trap from the kitchen sink when he heard the explosion inside the house. That coupled with my Mama hollering (she never screamed, just hollered) bolted him up the back porch steps into the carnage. Our kitchen had blood red trimmed cabinets with the black spade shaped handles that, up until that day, were spic and spanned to my Mama's OCD – cleanliness. When Daddy tore open the back screen door, he blanched. There in the middle of her haven, Mama stood covered in what he thought were her entire 10 pints of human blood.

She had been canning tomato soup stock for the upcoming winter in her pressure cooker on the front burner of our gas

My Mama

Caloric white enameled stove. The whole kitchen now matched the cabinet trim, and so did Mama. The Ball quart canning jars had launched out of the Enola Gay pressure cooker, landed on gray and red streaked linoleum tiles and exploded. Her legs had been cut by the shrapnel, and blood-drive hemoglobin puddled around her favorite Naturalizer open toe sandals. The ceiling, walls and her upper body were smeared in cooked Big Boy and Better Big Boy tomatoes. My Daddy thought the explosion had ruptured every vein in her calico aproned body. She stood there shell shocked. He was too, but he had been born too early for WWI and missed WWII because he was head of the household. This was comparable to a scene from the front lines, a rural *Red Badge of Courage.*

That's about all my sisters and I know of the telling and re-telling of the reason we younguns couldn't be in the kitchen when Mama was using her pressure cooker. When that little stainless steel cylinder, perched on the escape valve of the cooker's lid, started to bobble and spit steam, that was our instructed exit to "Go play in the yard!" How the two of them cleaned up the mess and dealt with Mama's cut legs was a blurred epilogue. "Putting by" for the winter sometimes meant facing culinary danger, and Mama was a kitchen soldier with war wounds to prove it.

When we parceled out her kitchen wares after she died, the pressure cooker sat there like an artifact from some lost civilization. No one wanted it or knew how to use it. But it represented the obsession of our Mama to have food on the table when the gardens were gone, and you never knew if the next winter might repeat the Great Depression.

Nowadays, my sisters both replicate that soup stock without a pressure cooker. But we all know it's "almost" as good as Mama's; we just don't talk to each other as we enjoy it.

Funny how I look at Ball jars in antique shops or at yard sales and still try to imagine that sound that brought my Daddy from his appointed task. I can almost hear it in the middle of February at either one of my sister's houses as we eat their homemade soup. But it's as distant and faint as that ghostly sound that steals down a chimney long after the last sparks have joined the stars.

After I was grown and moved away, I would spend my summers with my parents. Daddy would unlock the sacred cupboard in the utility room that held the canned summer gardens. We would dump jars and jars of two and three year old canned soup stock that had turned a strange shade of bleached mud. Mama needed more jars. The shelf space was limited, but never less than full. She didn't have to date any jars. She could tell the year by the faded shade of red.

Precaution was an understatement about Mama. Her ounce of prevention bordered on witch doctory. One day I was riding behind my sister, Celia, on her bicycle and my foot slipped off the little knob on the hub that a back rider precariously trusts. I was barefooted of course, and the next thing I knew my right heel was being planed like a rough cut pine plank into a polished table top. The odd thing about that maneuver was that it hurt like all get out, but there was no blood. The spokes had peeled

3

the skin off my Achilles tendon, and all you could see was the pearl white of my heel's pulley system. I went yelling into the house and ran up to my Mama in the kitchen. She didn't have time for distraction. This was in the 50s when screw worms were the scourge to cattle farmers. Screw worms were the maggot-like larvae of the screw worm fly that laid its eggs in open wounds and ate their way from inside out. They were eradicated by a federal project that released irradiated sterile male flies from airplanes across the affected parts of the US. My Daddy had this purple gloopy concoction furnished by the county extension service that he lathered on any sore or cut or scrape that showed up on his cows, dogs, or mules.

Well Mama, without so much as a "Poor Child!" went to the barn, got the veterinary poultice, sat me down, told me to "Hush!" and slathered the kerosene smelling slop on my heel. No child of hers was going to get screw worms.

I stopped crying because the burning flooded my whimpering boy frame like I had been stung by a convention of red velvet ants whose guests were one thousand guinea wasps. Nothing since has reached that threshold of pain, though my later described circumcision at the age of 12 came close.

I think I must have lost uncounted days due to the shock, but no screw worms took up residence in my heel. I still have the scar which is shaped like the continent of Africa drawn by a myopic shaman. Apropos.

Achilles had to deal with a mere arrow. If my Mama had been around back then, we'd be short of that cautious myth. She would have had the power to rewrite history, one heel at a time.

And then there were my knees. I enjoyed playing in the dirt as much as a mule wallowing in a dusty barnyard in the middle of a rainless July. Short pants, shoeless, and a pullover shirt from Bedsole Dry Goods Co. in Thomasville were my play clothes. I knelt in the barren landscape of a grassless southern frontier which grownups around me called a backyard, and shot marbles with Junior or steered my toy cars on roads he and I had scraped with a hoe into patterns of senseless civil engineering. Junior always wore long pants so he was protected from the plague that attacked boy knees. Ring worms. Until I got my degree in biology, I was reluctant to admit they were not worms, but a skin fungus due to playing in dirt. Mama's treatment left mental and physical scars.

I was scrubbed all over at the end of a summer day like a desilked ear of Silver Queen corn. My knees got a second serious scrubbing with Octagon soap and a brush that was probably a bonus gift from the Stanley salesman who came by the house and sold brushes for every occasion out the back of his station wagon. "Got a boy with ring worm on his knees?" I'm sure he said. "Sure do!" said my Mama. "Need a course one that removes several layers of skin

Mama & Her sister Lupearl

quickly?" he interpreted from that "Sure do!" Today we call them wire brushes which remove layers of oil base paint from window shutters or the clapboard planking of old country houses that have been painted and repainted since the dawn of creation. Hyperbole.

Red skin was clean skin and next to raw was mere preparation for her cure. Clean as a whistle and laid out on a white percale sun dried sheet, my Mama would prepare the body. Mummification of the Pharaohs paled in comparison.

My Daddy initiated the ritual by cutting in half unripe

(green) black walnuts placed precisely in his red handled vice at the end of his carpenters table. The exact halves fell into a white enameled pan on the ground that also collected the tobacco brown juice that dripped out of the walnuts as he severed the orbs. Like ancient Egyptian embalmers, he delivered the unguent to rid the body of ringworm afterlife. On my near bleeding knees, with their pinkish circles of "worms," Mama placed an oozing half of the tannic acid remedy. Tannic acid is exactly what it sounds like. Acid can be used to dissolve anything from mortar off bricks to the complete disappearance of a penny or nickel or an innocent boy's kneecaps. Not hyperbole.

I was not allowed to move or the walnut juice would get on the sheet which I'm sure could be cleaned by some bleach concoction that Mama had hidden in her medieval medicine cabinet, probably made from spittle bug foam she had collected at midnight from the Johnson grass growing around the fence of our cemetery.

Don't squirm, don't cry, don't dare open your eyes. Lying there was my "Cast of Amontillado." I was walled in black pain on the brightest summer days since the big bang. It took hours. A minute is an hour when you're being treated by your alchemist mother.

Where the ring worms had been were now burnt sienna discs, like hieroglyph tattoos that faded sometime way into my adolescence. When the winter came that year, as my tan legs paled around them, they spotted my knees with subcutaneous reminders that contact with the ground held the promise of pain at the end of road trips across my grassless frontier.

Without books, she had figured out answers that caused me to want to know the questions. She taught me that you didn't need a pound of cure, just that proverbial ounce.

Pain was just relative.

6

2

Blue is for boys

The tragic scene has been described to me at family gatherings, be it a holiday or a visit from a relative we haven't seen in a month of Sundays. What brings it up can be anything from telephone party lines to missing the joy of cold fresh buttermilk (which no one has any more unless you're stuck somewhere in time on a dairy farm in a Mennonite community in south-eastern Tennessee).

I, the victim, was in that period of life labeled "just a baby." The versions vary from "who saw what" to "I know what happened." And I simply accept them as variations on my Lazarus Luck.

My oldest sister, Celia, was rocking me in her lap and either fell asleep or was distracted by any number of things an eight year old girl has going on in her head. It might have been a dirt dobber she saw building its mud pipe organ house on the side porch, a nest of red ochre from upturned road dirt brought in by the county road crew to stop the washboard ruts in front of our house. These mud artists can rival the chevron patterns of my grandmother's Afghans with just nature and spit and ground.

Anyway, I slid head first out of her lap and my soft spot was the first body part to find the heart pine floor of our old house. The malleable skull of a three month old and the marble hardness of heartwood pine produced what is generally described as being "knocked out." The color-wheel shades described in my "turning blue" ranges from simple "Robin's egg" to "somewhere between eggplant and Grapico." (As a Tennessee Williams fan, I'd like to think it was "Della Robbia.") Celia screams, gets Mama, Mama dials for someone to help (there were no doctors with in twenty miles) and I euphorically was floating somewhere in the innocent, limbo land of baby brain asphyxiation. In other words "out like a light!" and changing colors faster than a last minute Easter egg dye job.

Marie Singleton, our cousin who my mother claimed never put the telephone down (there were seven on our party line), hears the pleas and rushes up to our house, storms through the door and, so the story goes, dashes to the icebox, grabs what she thinks is a pitcher of water to, God knows, either shock me back into existence or baptize me before I had even "known" Jesus. To this day, I can't figure out the logic. They say I sputtered back to life, spitting up the thickly balm. I turned a lovely shade of primrose and smiled and rolled around in the lactic Sea of Galilee.

Of course it wasn't a pitcher of water; it was fresh buttermilk.

Whether or not I made baby angels as I flapped my pudgy arms in the white puddle, I haven't the slightest, but I do know when I was weaned off my Mama's nipples and into my toddler years, there was nothing better than a cold glass of fresh buttermilk from one of our Jersey cows and my Mama's corn bread crumbled up in it, redefining "mother's milk."

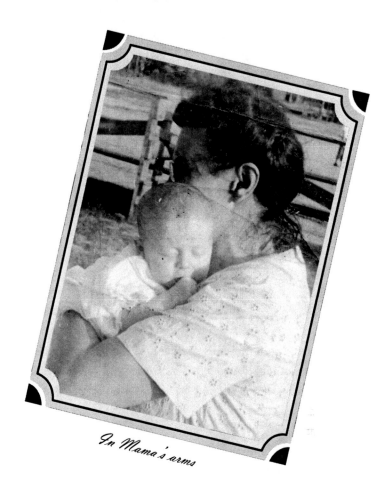

In Mama's arms

3

Jesus was my older brother

My mother and father were the most devout two people on the planet. They were perfect. Absolutely perfect. Forget the Pope; forget Billy Graham. My father was the head of the deacons at Putnam Baptist Church. For 50 plus years he served. Somewhere I have that plaque that is inscribed with the proof of his sainthood; I was at the ceremony.

Summers. Revivals. Meals with visiting preachers. Sometimes they were humans; sometimes they were backward hollerers by whom the revival committee had been fooled into believing they had witnessed a man of God, but turned out they had seen him on his *best* day. We suffered the fools.

Because of my Daddy's seniority among the deacons, he got to choose which day Mama had to cook for the preacher. Every day, dinner and supper were parceled out to various wives of deacons who were all vying for sainthood. Their special foods, as proof of the blessing by the visiting "man of God," were required for acceptance into heaven. Food was as good as communion. And Mama's famous chicken salad – oh my God, her chicken salad – sure beat those stale, soggy, saltine bits we ate for Jesus' body. It always confused me that so little a piece of cracker was enough to get you into heaven. I loved large helpings. Still do.

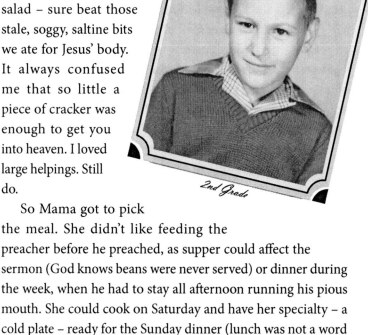

2nd Grade

So Mama got to pick the meal. She didn't like feeding the preacher before he preached, as supper could affect the sermon (God knows beans were never served) or dinner during the week, when he had to stay all afternoon running his pious mouth. She could cook on Saturday and have her specialty – a cold plate – ready for the Sunday dinner (lunch was not a word that existed in Putnam unless it was packed with a Thermos for work, or if you were too poor for school lunches and had to take that embarrassing, greasy, reused brown paper bag on the bus to be pointed and snickered at). And so, after an entire week of running the preacher all over town to various events, Mama was just plain tired of him and a cold plate send-off was a kind of good-riddance. She was very critical (unlike my benevolent Daddy) of preacher styles and their downright commonness.

Well, we had a doozy this particular summer. Not only was he loud, he smelled like a smokehouse. A smokehouse is where you cure meat and its smell is somewhere between rancid and just plain nasty. That was him. I could tell Mama wanted him in-and-out of the house before his odor soaked into the tablecloth. Mama had dinner all ready before church that morning: the chicken salad, potato salad, ham, pickled peaches, Ritz crackers and her equally spectacular pear salads with their Del Monte pear halves nestled in an Iceburg lettuce leaf with a mound of shredded commodity hoop cheese on a glob of Blue Plate mayonnaise, and of course, the whole, not half maraschino cherry on top. And you ate this first. Heaven. She always waited to add the cherry after we got home from church so the red dye wouldn't color the mayonnaise. God was in her details.

And because it was summer and there were flies, she always turned the plates upside down on the table, just in case there had been one or two that had escaped her deadly flyswatter, a weapon that she wielded like a scimitar across the July air. And so when we got home, we immediately washed up, sat down, and after the blessing that we always hoped would be short, waited for the preacher to turn the first plate over.

Now it had never occurred to my family that a preacher could be so stupid as to not notice the word "Noritake" staring up at him from the bottom of the plate. But God must have been busy the day they gave brains to that Christian cretin. He had already put the entire congregation into apoplexy one night while spouting some verse of damnation and his upper plate of false teeth came flying out of his mouth and with no skip in his rant, he grabbed it out of the air like a line drive and popped it back into his head at the end of a one-syllable word, which he had a wealth of.

We should have known.

The usual protocol was that my Daddy would start the servings. But not this day in infamy. The preacher grabbed the chicken salad, got a big spoonful and while still running his prideful – and spittle-producing mouth, slapped a glob of salad smack down on the bottom of his plate. My world suddenly shifted on its axis. Looking at Mama with a mixture of shock and glee, my sisters and I waited. As the bowl came frighteningly near us (I was stationed just to the left of the dolt from Dropout Revival School) I waited for guidance. It came. My Mama, whose middle name was Dignity, looked at me, and, saying nothing, simply nodded her head in a way that spoke volumes, indicating that I was to do as the preacher did. The two things I remember most were: one; the tiny, tiny area on the bottom of my plate that had to hold all my sustenance (there was room for only one pickled peach, dammit!) and two; the deafening silence underneath the idiot's jovial cluelessness.

As the bowl passed, the chicken salad went PLOP on my sisters' plates, PLOP on my Daddy's plate and what

13

seemed like the quietest moment in the universe, *plop* on my mother's plate. Our eyes were as big as moons by this time, but as each bowl of manna passed, she would look at us, and there would be the subtle nod that was a cross between a neck stretch and a prayer nod. We knew. There it was right in front of each of us. Small tapas servings of dignity, humanity, altruism and... obedience. So came my greatest lesson in life to that point: when your mother nods, you put anything you have "on the back of the plate."

When she served the lemon icebox pie, after we had stacked the impossible-to-pick-up plates and taken them into the kitchen, we knew what to expect. There they were, those perfect slices of yellow joy topped off with tanned meringue and crowned with those small beads of amber sweetness... on the bottoms of the dessert plates. Ironically the slices looked gigantic.

The dead get all the pretty flowers

My older brother lived for only four days. His tombstone says: T. W. Harris, Jr. Feb. 10, 1934; and Feb. 14, 1934. Mama said he died after scratching his perfect milk glass cheek and bleeding to death as she and Daddy watched. She simply called him a "bleeder." There was no car, no phone, and, we later learned, no support from my father's father. It was the Great Depression. Daddy had married "beneath" him, and he and my Mama were estranged from his parents for three years. All this I learned not long before my Mama died in 1994. It was not something anyone was proud of or talked about, or even needed to talk about. I think she finally had forgiven my grandfather, but there wasn't much love lost. After all, that small two and a half foot slab of marble with its hard baby pillow inscribed with just the name and dates always was lying there in the cemetery to remind her. If only they had had a car. Or maybe just a little forgiveness. But anyway...

On Decoration Day in May, the living smothered the dead with flowers that were too beautiful to live very long. Daddy was the chief custodian of the cemetery, and when I was small, way before garish plastic flowers, he had to throw away the wilted, sad, too- expensive mums and glads and roses a week after the ceremony. I went with him sometimes, and it always broke my heart to see there in the hot, May sun the rot of flowers denied water and marked with tags professing love and remembrance – for a week at the most. Somehow, I always thought of them as dead as they were placed on the graves on that Sunday in May. The roses always died first. I thought of Decoration Day as a kinda weird birthday party for my dead brother. I had never known him, of course, but somehow thought he was so special – only four days old – that he got to go live with Jesus before me. Mama said he went to live with Jesus, so I assumed Jesus was a relative, probably a much older brother. My brother's little marble slab was so cool in the post-church sun that I would lie down on it. For some reason known only to my Mama and Daddy, I was never asked to get up. I remember the taste of the marble if I licked it and how the slick

My older brother's grave

surface reflected the clouds. It was as if his blue playground in the sky moved slowly across the shine. He was of course in Heaven. It was somehow comforting to lie there. As if he knew I was his brother.

I was very strange as a child. Sometimes a relative, say from Mobile, or somewhere far off like Mississippi, would take a picture of me lying there. "How sweet," they whispered. "How weird," was what they, I'm sure, were thinking. Just Ronald. Everyone knew Ronald was "different." But I was always dressed so spiffy that those pictures probably are in some album, dog-eared for quick reference, to show how once we revered the dead to the point of true excessiveness. A small, sweet boy, curled up with his brother and a number of white carnations – such a Kodak moment.

He was born & three months later He died

Jesus, God, and that unfathomable Holy Spirit were all like relatives that you hoped would never really visit when you were young. There were pictures; you knew what they looked like; but you never felt like you'd be dressed properly if they showed up. Much less be ready with all your sins somewhere in remission. When I was in my early teens, I always hoped I'd get a little more time before He came again. Mama and Daddy, of course, wanted to see Him. They were ready. I figured if I got to be as old as they were, somewhere in their early 50s, I'd have my heaven bags packed. I'm 65 now. An overnight kit is all I've packed so far.

But I sure did love Him when I was floating in that world

18

my parents painted of His love and His perfection. The framed portraits in my Sunday school rooms as Beginners, Intermediates, and Young People all made Him look like He knew me, and I always wanted Him to turn towards me (some reason He was always in profile), and say "Hello." I really had this pure feeling that He had heard all my prayers. If he just would turn around and say "Hello." My house is filled with Jesus memorabilia. Reminders of my once Baptist innocence.

He had two big days out of the year that were just for Him.

I always was good at decorating, so the Christmas tree at church was my territory. The pulpit area was so high we could cut monsters in my Daddy's woods. Big as two of our house trees. Fatter, thicker, taller. A green "smell-so-good-canvas" I could paint on until it looked visibly pained – more was more for Baby Jesus. The church had years of Christmas decorations saved up and nothing matched, and it didn't matter. It was His birthday party. Big event. Everybody had been invited.

We exchanged gifts at the church. Everybody brought a "man" gift and "woman" gift, and they were handed out to everyone there. Leftovers were given to the poor, the invalids, the drunks. It was the only time of the year my Mama would allow her Christian heart to sympathize with a town drunk. They were damned for the 364 other days. But she had reasons. There's the time three drunk brothers ripped the shirt off Daddy when he tried to kick them out of my grandfather's store. Or the time one wrecked his car, turned it over, and laughed when

7th Grade

my father got to the scene. He was so drunk that he'd forgotten his boys were trapped in the car. When Daddy got him home his wife, pale and quiet, asked about the boys. Daddy flew back and found them crying in the wreck. They were so scared of their drunk father, they wouldn't make a sound when he was around. I remember being with my father, and when we found them, the tires on the upside down car were still spinning. I swear I remember this.

That's why my Mama hated drunks. Never forgave them. The love-thy-neighbor thing stopped at the bottle. Dead stop. But at the gift giving, His birthday softened her heart.

For years I trimmed the tree and sang next to my mother and father on their pew – second from the front on the left – the songs we all knew. I still hear her alto voice in my head when they're played. She sweetened the air with her harmony. I never could do harmony. I only wanted to hear hers. I still do.

The other holiday, Easter, was the worst day of the year for me. Why did He have to die just three months after He was born? How did he become 33 in three months? I had trouble with time in those days.

New clothes didn't matter. Colored eggs, peeps, cellophane in blinding hues, and chocolate bunnies couldn't hide Jesus' pain. Why eggs? Why bunnies? Still not clear to me. Something about eggs delivered by clergy in England? Something about rabbits left on doorsteps? Jesus dying, and marshmallow peeps with black BB eyes tasting like sweet chewy meringue somehow didn't compute into reason. I ate the peeps' BB eyes first, then the head, then the rest. I ate with anger that tasted sorta crazy sweet. It was the beginning of the end of Ronald's innocence. It ended completely the day I rode into "Jerusalem" on my "donkey."

It was Palm Sunday and it was the last day our cows stayed in my Daddy's pasture. My grandfather had a pasture about two miles up the road, through town, past the church, and on up a dirt road. When our cows had eaten all the new growth, they were herded up the road to Big Daddy's. Smokey, my Shetland pony, was their guide. They followed him everywhere. Daddy usually hooked him up to the pick up and slowly drove the annual trek. The cows never strayed. They were on their way to greener pasture.

I felt metaphorical that day and decided to dress as Jesus on His donkey going into Jerusalem. Daddy had no idea what I had in mind, but just past the house with all the devoted-to-Smokey cows following, I took out two of Mama's sheets I had secretly placed under me as a "saddle," and wrapped myself in Biblical remnants and head gear and all that matched the picture in our Young Peoples' classroom at church. Imagine the sight of a bed-sheeted silly teenage boy on his pony, followed by twenty-five or thirty cows, slowly traveling a dirt road through a town that consisted of two general stores across from each other, a post office, and a couple of houses. I thought it was the most brilliant act I had accomplished up to that point in my life.

What I didn't realize was that even though my folks heard about it, never saying a word to me, that I had somehow overstepped the line from respect into acting, and perhaps maybe, just maybe, I had done Jesus a disservice. I was different after that day. Not tangible different, just different. The next Friday, as always, He died.

And for the first time, the literal vanished and I knew He was never supposed to turn His head and say "Hello."

Christmas 1957

21

6

Number three washtubs

Junior McGrew was my best friend for what seemed like a lifetime, because days of summer were more than 24 hours. During schooldays, Junior rode the black bus and I rode the white bus and I would get off at his house to spend the afternoon. Mama knew where I was if the bus passed our house without stopping. There never seemed to be a worry. Granny, Junior's Mama, would have something on her black iron wood-burning stove for us to eat. Sometimes I would stay for supper. Their house was on our property and they paid no rent. Granny washed and ironed for my Mama. I guess you could say we had servants, but that's totally wrong. They were family. I didn't even think about Junior being black. He was

22

just Junior – my best friend. We didn't know about integration or segregation. We were so far out in the country that one of the biggest events in our lives was when a Greyhound Bus got lost and came through Putnam. We had dirt roads. The sight of that bus whooshing through Putnam, followed by a long cloud of dust was like a land-locked comet filled with people from somewhere going somewhere else. We were that isolated. That bus became a constant point of reference as I grew up. I sometimes wonder if the people on that bus might remember me standing in our front yard with Junior, staring at them. We were the monkeys at the zoo. They were paying customers.

The tubs.

Summer. Granny washed on Mondays. I don't know why. But there were three sizes of tubs. Number three for the first wash. Number two for the first rinse and number one for the second rinse. We had a shallow well, so we couldn't waste water. The clothes came from the black wash pot where they were boiled. Wood burned under the pot. Now this is summer, but the tradition of white, I mean white, clothes mattered to my Mama. So the fire was just plain necessary.

There was a liquid called "bluing" that was poured into the pot. This stuff had the weirdest smell I have ever smelled, but it made sheets so white that they rivaled the nimbus behind Jesus's head. And hanging on the line, my God, they smelled so good that bumblebees would light all over them thinking they were gardenias or something. Junior and I thumped them off. From a distance they looked like bullet holes.

After the wash, Mama and Granny would fill the tubs with water and put them out around in the yard and at the end of the day, after playing, the sun would have warmed the water and me and Junior and his brothers, Doog, Lemar and Coy would strip down naked to wash off the day's dirt. Soaping up

Junior's hair was my favorite thing. His wooly hair made suds as big as mountains. I would sculpt art pieces on top of his head: spikes, arches, waves. Thank God this took place in the back yard. Picture a skinny, naked, white boy playing hairdresser to a sudsy, naked Negro boy in a number three washtub with his brothers sitting in their tubs as contestants number two and number three. Well, maybe you don't need to picture it. All I know is it was my first Art 101 class.

Then we would rinse off with the hose that had been lying in the sun all afternoon. Get dressed and in my high from creating soap art, we would play "Sling Statue," our last thing before they went home. It's like "Popping-the-Whip." Wherever they landed they would freeze. Weird positions, mostly on the ground, and I would judge who had the best "statue." I guess I was something of an art tyrant. I don't remember anyone slinging me. Maybe that's why I became a teacher.

So, that was summer. In the fall, it was deer season. Our yard was always where the deer were brought to be skinned and cut up. Daddy would have pulleys and ropes and single trees hung from our privet hedges for the deer. Single trees are the wooden bars with hooks on the ends that you used to guide the mule down the rows in the garden or cotton fields. Ropes were looped to the metal hooks on the ends and you could get the mule to "gee" or "haw" by pulling right or left. The metal hooks were threaded through the Achilles tendons of the deer's back legs and strung up to be cut open. A big kitchen butcher knife split the deer wide open from groin to throat and the guts fell out into number three washtubs to keep from getting dirt on them. You had to be careful not to cut the gall bladder 'cause the bile would spoil the meat. The dogs got the guts. I can remember alpha dogs – I didn't know about alpha dogs then, I just knew they were the meanest ones that got the first helpings. I can still remember the smell and the steam coming off the washtubs with dogs sometimes in the tubs, growling and gorging.

These tubs were used so much for so many things that sometimes Daddy would have separate places for them: ones with holes in the bottom we used to get tomatoes or potatoes or squash or peas or whatever from the garden, rusty ones were in the barn for corn or dry peas and new ones were for clothes and me and Junior. They hung on nails all around the wash shed or pump house. Some were so old, hens nested in them. We never threw one away.

I stopped getting bathed in them because of one Christmas. Daddy was always the first person anyone called when there was trouble. One time one of our town drunks rounded the corner from Highway 69 to the church and fell out of the car and rolled into a ditch and the car crashed into a big oak in front of the church. Daddy was called. He took the drunk home and had his car towed home. Daddy never judged people, just took them home.

Anyway, one Christmas day he got a call that there had been a car wreck on Horse Creek Bridge. I saw him get the tubs, stack them in the trunk of the car and, for some reason, told me to come along.

A car had tried to pass another on the bridge and cut back too soon, crashing the car into the bridge railing. Now Horse Creek Bridge is about a quarter of a mile long. The car, instead of going over the railing, rode the railing at high speed for a long time, and the railing, which is sharp galvanized steel, sliced the car down the middle and peeled it open like a watermelon chopped by a machete. And it chopped open the people inside, too. It was filled with a black family. We stopped at the end of the bridge and I can remember Daddy walking around the end of the bridge with the tubs. I had no idea why he was doing this.

I got out of the car and looked over the railing and there was Daddy, carefully placing the tubs over severed body parts. I saw one and got sick and got back in the car. The next day, the day after Christmas, I looked out at the wash shed and there the tubs were, hung where they had always hung, clean and silver. The next summer I told my Mama I was too big to bathe in the tubs. I couldn't stand the thought of getting into those tubs. I heard later on after the accident, that one of our tubs had been placed over a severed head.

I remember being glad Junior's family didn't have a car.

7

Growing up on highway 69:
The icecream man & the green
Dotted Swiss recital dress

I was in the second grade when the incident with the ice cream man and the green Dotted Swiss recital dress happened. My parents owned a general store that shared space with the post office just across the road from our house. My sisters played piano and took lessons from Miss Evalee Singleton, a spinster that smelled of lavender and gardenias. I remember her smell because I waited in her classroom for my sisters to finish their piano lessons. I sat with my sisters on the bus ride home.

We had a piano in the living room because my Mama at one time knew how to play it. I don't remember ever hearing her play it, but my Mama never lied. So there were the endless

27

recitals, and my oldest sister's recital dresses, which Mama made, were handed down to my youngest sister. There was this one particular one which I was – for want of a better word

– attracted to. It was green and it was made out of Dotted Swiss. I think I loved it because Dotted Swiss is very tactile. When you touch it, it has those little bumps, those little raised dots on it that just fascinated me. How did they make that? My sisters kept it in a long box underneath the bed and it was like, you know, the Holy of Holies. You don't touch it. You don't go there.

So when my parents were over at the post office, and hopefully my sisters were gone... I don't know where they were... dating... gone... I don't know and certainly didn't care, as long as they were gone. Well I would sneak into our room – we all slept in the same room – and get the box out from under their bed, and carefully take it out and put on the Dotted Swiss dress. The privacy of the room was very special. The dress! The dress! I remember soooo much about it. It was full circle and from the waist down it had these rows of ruffles every twelve inches. It was ankle length on my sisters so it was floor length on me. Oh my God... it was a gown. It was this beautiful green, somewhere between a sea foam and a turquoise green. (Years later I was at Sherwin-Williams looking at paint chips, and came across this green called Juliet's Poison, and suddenly that dress floated in front of me like a ghostly mist, and I almost had to catch myself from stumbling.) That dress, that color, that name – Juliet's Poison – that memory, that irony.

I put it on many times. And I got to where I took a lot of liberties. I went out of the house. I went into the backyard. I loved to twirl – the full skirt, the spinning – I didn't know about whirling dervishes in Turkey or anything – I knew nothing about dancing, but there was this sea of wonderfulness as I spun. I went to Turkey in 1999, and while watching a dervish turn madly, I felt a sudden rush of why they did it. I had done it as a second grader in my back yard in Putnam, Alabama. I had briefly seen God.

I didn't spin in the backyard often, but one day I was seeing God and I heard a horn blow. It was the ice cream truck from Selma that delivered those wonderful little paper tubs of ice cream with the flat wooden spoons that had that vinegar acid-like smell before you dipped them into a circle of cold heaven. Anyway, the horn blew its signal that the driver, named Johnny George, created special for my Daddy. One long blast followed by two short beep-beeps. I stopped, but it wasn't the ice cream that I wanted, it was something far more special. Since my Daddy sold a lot of ice cream, Johnny George would bring him these 8 x 10 colored pictures of movie stars. I don't know why. Promotions. Pin ups. Who knows. But I loved them. And my sisters got them, never me. These pictures were the first time I learned that there was a world outside of Putnam. Nobody in Putnam looked like Ester Williams, leaning up against what looked like to me a real pier piling with the rope wrapped around it and her hands behind her and her one piece bathing suit with the panel across her privates – and with the little Janzen diving girl logo. That little bathing capped girl killed me. Anyway I loved those picutres. One was Nancy Olsen – who was Nancy Olsen? I don't know why I remember her, but those pictures and the green Dotted

Swiss dress were like my favorite things. So that day, wearing that dress, hearing the horn, losing what little mind I had at that age, I ran across the road. To the post office. I don't know if my mother knew or suspected or even entertained the idea that I twirled in the backyard in my sister's recital dress, but running across the road was something she would not have wanted to happen. Not to mention my father!

So I ran up to Johnny George who was giving the ice cream boxes to my father and I was so excited and winded, and as politely as a boy in a dress could say to an older man, I said, "Do you have any of the pictures?" There I was in the green Dotted Swiss and him in his green delivery uniform and he said, after a glance at my mother, then my father, "I usually give them to your... sisters." There was another pause, more glances, and he finally said, after reaching in his satchel, "Here, you can have them."

Easter 1951

I didn't know I was in the dress, I just knew I wanted those pictures. I grabbed them, thanked him, and ran back across the road. When I got over there I was looking at my treasure spread out on the edge of the back porch, looked down and realized, Ohhhhh... in the dress, in front of my mother, my father, and Johnny George, and... the world.

30

It was out, no secrets anymore. I took off the dress, put it carefully back in the box. But the pictures were mine. They were mine. Ester Williams was mine.

Later that day my mother said, "Ronald, if you're going to wear the dress, don't come across the road."

Epilogue: About, I don't know, fifteen years ago, we were in Selma – our doctors were in Selma, my parents were getting very old and we always ate at The Downtowner Cafe. We were in there that day and my mother said, "Why, there's Johnny George!" And he came over to the table. "Mr. and Mrs. Harris how are you?" and "Fine!" and whatever they said. "This is our son, Ronald." And he looked at me and after an abnormally long pause, he said, "Yes, I remember you. You still favor your sisters."

8

Junior was as black as a rotary dial phone

*I*didn't know he was black. I mean, in a race kinda way. I knew he was so shiny. I thought sometimes I saw myself reflected in his face. What it really was, was I wanted desperately to be his color. Black like soot that fell out of the chimney when Daddy cleaned it each spring. Black like the night just before the first birds sing in the morning – around 4 a.m. Black that absorbed the light and let it seep way down into his soul to light up his laughter. His laugh ripped open the day and let hours turn into long whole weeks, whole clock-stopping summers just this short of time-travel. His love for me and mine for him was so complete and real, I sometimes think back and wonder if he was imaginary.

I saw him any afternoon I wanted during the school year. And whole summers were his and mine. Our folks let us be whoever and whatever we created and never called us home until it started to get dark. He slept on a pallet next to my bed and we bathed in number 3 wash tubs in warm summer, clear water from our shallow well. The number 3 in the center of the bottom of the tub was wavery and loopy as we stepped into the circle of warmth and wetness. I don't remember him ever calling my name, and I only said his name when he was not there. We didn't need to address each other. We just... were.

For 16 years we hung around. He had three brothers: Doog, Lemar, Coy, and one sister, Jenny. We broke Doog's arm one day playing over at his house. We pretended his brothers were dolls that we carried around, propped on window sills, or dressed up in clothes we found lying around. Doog was a "window doll" one day, and they would (probably at my bossy insistence) remain still till we changed their positions, or created weird tableaus of boy "dolls" having tea or jumbled in heaps of abandonment. Junior and I had young screwed-up imaginations. Maybe our parents should have checked up on us more often.

Anyway, Doog was not cooperating that day, so Junior and I looked at each other, a sinister thought gave birth at the same time in our brains, and we just pushed Doog gently out the window. His crying never stopped us all day from continuing to arrange him in positions to teach him a lesson.

At the end of the day, when his Mama, Granny, came home, she realized a small bone was sticking out of his arm, and the arm had swollen to twice its size. We were beaten by respective Mamas and never got to play that twisted game again. At least not with Doog. Lemar was always game, but no window sills. I somehow remember we always put Lemar in a dress. If I could find him today, I'd like to see if he remembers our proclivities.

33

Maybe he's blocked it out. Thank God. Poor Doog. I'm sure his children never got to play with white children. Lemar wore dresses well, I recall.

Somehow my most vivid memories of Junior always ended up with a whippin'. Not a spanking – a whippin', because our adventures escalated into Grand Guignol types with endings so spectacular, punishment – and I mean "lesson-learning" punishment – was called for.

We had no grass in our half-acre yard. Every sprig was scraped with hoes, brushed with brush brooms to smooth out the dirt, and finally scraped with a garden rake, the kind with the iron teeth,

Me & Junior 1959

into designs that would make a Buddhist Monk's Mandela pale. And then the destruction began. Junior and I would each get a hoe and scrape smooth roads crisscrossing in the yard until we met. And there at that point, sometimes as many as ten points, a vast volcano would mount up with the collected dirt of our road making. Mounds of dirt, rivaling Mount Etna or Vesuvius. And begging to top them off would be empty Vienna sausage cans, brimming with kerosene.

Now, this only happened on days that Mama and Daddy were gone, or in the garden, or somewhere that an hour or two was left to the dangerous duo of Ronald and Junior. Kerosene was forbidden to touch, therefore it was desirable. Gasoline was such a no-no that we dared only to dip our shoe laces or a piece of rope in the gas can, and connect the Vienna sausage can in the caldera down the backside of the volcano to Junior, some kitchen matches, and his big grin.

I was always the traveler along the new roads, oblivious that I was in volcano country. As I sang or whistled along in my plastic convertible car I'd gotten at the Five & Dime in Selma, I pretended to stop and marvel at the dormant volcano. As I was singing of the joy of the earth, Junior would light the shoelace or rope and it quickly shot up to the kerosene, which plopped (kerosene plops, not pops) into flame, and I would scream with faux-fear as the unthinkable would happen. Junior took the hoe handle and nudged the can to spill its fire and death onto my singing idiocy, and my perfectly meltable vacation car. As it curled and puddled into stinking aquamarine colored muck, I would choke out death throws as I writhed in the dirt, twitching as the flames charred me in my imagination. Then, when the last of the plastic car popped or sizzled, there would be the obligatory silence. Then, as if we were having seizures, we would laugh and run around and grab each other in a boy-madness, that if witnessed would have meant confinement at Partlow, Alabama's mental hospital for children.

We did this charade twice. Once, we had time to clean up all the evidence of "nature's violence," but the second time we didn't get past that obligatory silence. Daddy appeared. He whipped me first, and then Junior. Granny would have killed Junior. My father was a gentler executioner.

We looked at our cars differently after that. We traveled new yard roads, but it was always across safer territory. Flatlands of Texas or Australia. We never took roads that made us laugh out loud again. But we remembered our vacation where I "died," and it was our favorite we took together. Also, our shoes stayed on better after that wonderful day, even though we didn't really notice. Trouble is, we had to find more forbidden forays. How quickly we forgot our sore backsides.

My sisters had a doll stove that I was never allowed to touch. So of course, Junior and I took it into the backyard, built a huge fire in it by sticking lightwood sticks in its oven door. Lightwood (we called it "lightered")is what it says, it's pine stump wood so loaded in resin that it bursts into flames when a match is near it. They were always in a coal scuttle near our fireplace in the living room. Fabulous fire stuff, almost as good as kerosene. The doll stove's paint began to peel, and the fire got out of control. I was cooking my usual "turnips," which were grass and water in sardine cans, on all "burners." The burners peeled away. The plastic knobs melted into the "turnips," and we had a small bonfire.

In my fire fighting eight year old wisdom, I took a stick and tried to save my "dinner." The sardine can turned over into the inferno, and there was an immediate water-meets-hell smoke screen that obliterated Junior, who was standing behind the stove. He screamed as the scalding water hit his ankle, and I thought I had killed him. When I got to him, he was wide eyed and staring at his ankle. His black skin had changed to a pink jello, and I did what any best friend who had scalded his best friend would do. I passed out. It was the beginning of my defense against pain – mine or others – faint. I have tons of fainting stories.

When I came to, I was being whipped. That's always a cure for fainting! And Junior was gone. He wasn't as badly burned as it seemed. But he was a little distant to me for several weeks. His soul was so pure, he forgave my own dark, troubled, fire loving one. We never talked of the incident again, but there were no more fire adventures. Not with him at least.

I, knowing better, would always throw aerosol cans into the big oil barrel that we burned trash in, and watch the soot and ashes explode into the sky, and put out the grass that caught on fire around the can. That was nothing compared to the time I poured old cans of oil paint into the open flames of the barrel, and the explosion burned off my eyebrows and melted away my eyelashes. But that was private and scary as Hell. I think that was the last time with fire, and my warped program for attempted suicide. But then there was the fascination with electricity. That day, we really almost died.

The wire from the pump house to the meter box on the back porch was old, and began to lose its insulation. The naked wire gleamed in the sun. I imagined seeing the electricity in its shine. Daddy

Juniors old school house - today

was going to fix it, but he made sure Junior and I knew about its danger. Daddy forgot what idiots we were. Well, Junior wasn't simple minded, he was just afraid to hurt my feelings, even if it meant death for the both of us.

There was the long metal wire Daddy used to unstop the sewage drain, or unclog the underground clay pipes that led from the grease trap to its drain, into the pasture near the barn. It was long and straight and was just right for us to test the effects of electricity on the boy flesh of Ronald the Retardo, and Junior the Victim. We knew. Of course we knew. We wanted to die – well, I did. Junior's love was unconditional; he had no choice. I wanted especially to prove my Daddy wrong and be the first person to not ground electricity. To not be fried with brain-burning smoke coming out of my ears. Alas I was not the first.

We waited for the cat to be away. We waited for the summer of our discontent. We waited like sheep to the slaughter. We knew nothing of truisms. We were just bad children. We were about to reap the whirlwind.

I still wonder what caused us to want me to die. We both gripped the long cleaning wire by both hands, approached the naked strands of death, and slowly lowered it to an insulated patch to get our boy-courage up. And then we started to move it slightly towards the bare space, a few inches from our last resting place on earth.

And then the two wires connected.

Describing electrical shock doesn't require words. There are no words for it. Your brain is the only thing slightly working, and it's like bad, real bad. Dream falling onto knife points that keep cutting flesh that is as sensitive as eyelids. I remember jerking violently, smelling some kind of meat cooking, and then collapsing together with silence thick as sorghum molasses. The smell was our hair, our fingernails, our sin. Disobedience burns first and brightest. It smells the worst. It lingers in your mouth, like the smell of a drilled tooth, just after the pulp has been penetrated and that smoke rises out of your mouth, and settles back down on your tongue so you can taste the pain.

What had saved us was my Mama knocking the wire away with her brush broom. I was so weak from all the muscle contractions and the jerking that I welcomed her beating the crap out of me. I felt something close to normal. The pain she inflicted had a definite description, a familiar feel. It was real. It made me alive. I think I let her beat me for the first time with no resistance, no blame. I lay there in mea culpa, welcoming the pain. I probably tasted my tears and said, "How delicious." Contrition was never in my lexicon, but I really felt sorry for being a bad child that day. I don't remember what happened to Junior after the rescue, but I know he was, again, a stranger for weeks after that. Mama knew he was a victim of my rebellion and kept him far away from me. I was too young to be tried for murder. Premeditated murder. How she continued to love me was always a mystery.

I got better after that day in the electric chair. Several years went by before we plotted and schemed again. Funny how powerful disobedience punished by yourself can be. Wisdom follows stupidity revealed. My first learned truism.

Then Junior got one on me. I was petrified of the Boogerman upstairs. When I was punished, I was sent to the top of the stairs going to our second floor. My Daddy, who hand built our house, called it "a story and a half" cause the pitch of the roof cut the corners off the upstairs ceilings. They were my first evidence that off-center design is the most interesting. If my sisters had been involved in a spat and all three of us were separated, my oldest sister got the prime prison, the barn. I hated her more for being isolated in my favorite play place. My other sister's respite was the old outdoor toilet where all the old Sears Roebuck catalogues were stored. Figure why I hated her. Nothing was more fun to look at than those catalogues. Especially the Christmas collection, which was literally called "The Wish Book!"

No, I was sent to my Hell, the top of the stairs. The

Boogerman was hiding just around the half wall that surrounded the stairwell. He had a big appetite and I was the Blue Plate Special. I would feel his breath behind me and hear him smacking his lips. His favorite meat was young suckling bad children. I was always sent up there when he was the hungriest. I peed in my pants many times as I sat there, scared into civility. At least that was my parents' hope. From all accounts, I was the Devil's bastard step child. I would have upset even Hell. Or so they say.

One day Junior, knowing of my only weak spot, the Boogerman, slipped upstairs and hid behind a door after hearing Mama tell me to go upstairs and get something out of the cedar chest in the Long Room, It had three beds in it, it was that long. As I rounded the corner very fast, Junior leaped out and growled. I didn't even turn, for a strange orange curtain closed in front of my eyes as my legs turned to limp dish rags, and my soon-to-be-infamous "passing out" took place. He thought he had killed me, and he ran and got Mama, who was used to my antics. She slapped me awake, and as I looked at Junior, all ashen and scared, I for the first time realized how much I loved him. I wasn't mad. He had tried, in his way, to make me laugh, to have fun. I saw in his fear what I should have seen each time I had taken him to the brink of a disaster. He was a person, a very special human whom I treasured, took advantage of, and needed so very much. I don't think he ever understood why I didn't get mad at him. I hugged him and we played the rest of the day together in silence.

His "killing" me ended my death-wish adventures. We were growing up. Learning that decisions had consequences. That danger was not as attractive as before. The Boogerman also disappeared that day – completely. He had scared it out of me.

Thank you, Junior, for saving me from my fear of myself.

9

Aunt Sister & catching polio for twenty minutes

*A*unt Sister had a lot of money. And she could spend it as long as she kept up with every penny she spent. Uncle Dick was such a Scrooge that Aunt Sister had to keep a record of how much she paid for ice on vacations. (Daddy called her Sister so she was naturally our Aunt Sister.) After she died, a neighbor found her ledgers at a garbage dump in the swamp not far from Aunt Sister's house. I have them.

Way back in the 60s, when she traveled with her brother, Uncle Wallace, and his second wife, Lida Mae, she meticulously wrote in her embroidery like script – tight and fluid – a detailed listing of a paper cup and gum and even 37cents to the bellboy.

Her daily journals were so compact with details, it was as if she didn't write everything down then she didn't exist. Even on days she was sick and her weird tiny penmanship was shaky and broken, she recorded how many apple tarts she fried or how many pies she baked. Their house was a stop over for hunters, neighbors, relatives, and workers. Sick or not, she fed them. And then recorded the events. She slept very little. Got up at 1 a.m or 3 a.m and wrote or cooked or sewed. I still have more than a hundred letters she wrote me in college. Why did I save them? Maybe now I know.

Saturdays and summers were highlighted in my memory because of her. I got to go with her on her trips to Thomasville, the nearest town. Getting her hair fixed by Vera Bryan on the second floor of Bedsole Dry Goods Co. and then grocery shopping, was a typical Saturday. Daddy would drop me off early that morning at her house and I rode for about 30 minutes in their big Lincoln Town Car, the backseat a pasture of fancy upholstery, just sitting there smelling the richness. Aunt Sister would drop me off at the movie theatre, and buy me popcorn and a pickle and a Coca-Cola, and I lived the day in serial heaven. Over and over, riding with Roy Rodgers and Dale Evans and Gabby Hayes, and Superman flying me to his rescues, and Flash Gordon letting me zap various aliens that looked a lot like the Boogerman that lived upstairs at my house.

I always sat in the front row, and when she came to get me, the usher would call out, "Ronald Harris, your Aunt Sister is here!" Sometimes two or three times 'cause I was suspended somewhere in disbelief out west or at the Daily Planet.

One Saturday while I was lost in picture show heaven, like Brer Rabbit in the briar patch, my whole world, small and safe, shattered. The polio epidemic hung over my life like God's punishment for being a bad child. I thought you would be crippled by Him because you had not prayed or gone to church or because you'd peed in your bed. It was whispered, not said aloud ... polio ... like ... cancer ... or ... pregnant ... and I refused to acknowledge its existence. The only thing that smacked of reality were the horrible polio shots the county nurse wounded us with. Those needles were as big as a soda straw cut at an angle. I hated the county nurse so much that to this day when I smell white adhesive tape I feel faint.

The theatre where I caught polio - as it is today

The newsreel, close up and in stark black and white, with a voice over by the Angel of Death, always introduced the movies. I closed my eyes and chewed on the pickle. Well after so many repeats during the day, I snuck a peek. And there they were. The sinful children. The disobedient little hellions that had been stricken down in their badness with ... (whispered) polio. All in iron lungs. All looking up into those mirrors that stuck out of the top of the iron lung, reflecting their sad, pitiful, pale, sinful faces. As the Angel of Death talked and told us innocent victims in the dark to give our allowances to the March of Dimes and pray for a cure and count our lucky stars, something swept off the screen and hovered over me and went up my nose and into my soul, and because I had always some guilt for just existing ... I caught polio. You caught things in those days. Those pitiful

43

children's faces all floated about a foot above me and whispered, "You are a bad child. You deserve polio!" And I couldn't move my legs. I couldn't feel them. I had polio!

I began to cry. Then sob. Then melt down onto the cold tile floor and imagine the rest of my life in one of those large tin cans, forever staring into the mirror of guilt and punishment. I had no idea the iron lung was to help the breathing. I thought it was imprisonment for being bad.

I don't know what the others in the theatre thought, 'cause my world had ended. And then the usher called out, "Ronald Harris, your Aunt Sister is here!" Nothing would move. I had polio all over now. Not even my lips worked. I couldn't speak. No sound came out. I was completely polioed.

The usher yelled this time: "RONALD HARRIS, YOUR AUNT IS HERE AND SHE'S IN A HURRY!" Nothing. No whimper. No croak. Nothing. He came down the aisle, saw me huddled in polio and said, "Did you hear me? Your aunt…" He didn't finish the sentence. I had found some voice somewhere in the back of my throat, and whispered, "I have polio!" A moment. Then he leaned over and said in a surly tone, "Your aunt is going to beat you if you don't get up and go home!"

The next thing I knew they both were dragging me up the aisle with my legs splayed out behind me like a rag doll. God knows what the audience thought. I knew only that I had polio and I was destined for a black and white world of zombie children in long rows never getting to go to the picture show ever again. While being dragged up the aisle I remember looking back at the last movie of my life. I think it was Superman. He seemed to wave good-bye.

When we got outside, I was still Raggedy Andy until my Aunt Sister had had enough. She jerked me up, popped me upside the head and said, "Snap out of it. You're embarrassing me!" That did it. Her tone. Her eyes. Her slap.

I instantly was cured. My legs worked. My voice came back. I stammered, "I thought I had polio!" She looked at me like my second grade teacher, Mrs. Beddingfield, and said, "Everybody needs a little polio once in a while!"

The next year the Salk vaccine came out. The sugar cube sure beat those horse needles. But I always thought I didn't need any more vaccines. I had had polio for twenty minutes and I was totally immune.

When I 'caught' polio

10

Aunt Mary Cunningham & Uncle Tom Smith

Aunt Mary Cunningham smelled like the entire perfume counter at Sears at Christmas. She wore all her colognes at once. She also wore all her coats at once. All her jewelry. Sometimes, when she came up to my granddaddy's store, having caught a ride with anybody passing her house down on the Blue Rock river road, she'd have two or three of her hats on. She was just Aunt Mary Cunningham, and so we didn't say anything about her madness. Toothless, and at least one hundred and fifty years old, milk chocolate colored, and permanently giddy, she would grab me up in one of her layered hugs and I would get lost in all that fabric, scents, beads, silliness, and just about float away. Except she would hold on to me for about ten seconds too long. The combination of all that madness could take you close to suffocation, or even the possibility of osmosing into her body through the gabardine, wool, and osnaberg. The osnaberg (an unbleached cotton fabric with nubby brown flecks) was what most people made kitchen curtains out of. Aunt Mary Cunningham (it was never just "Aunt Mary") wore her kitchen curtains as a kind of shawl over the shoulders of her coats. July or January, she layered up. I don't know if she was afraid when she left home that it would burn down, or if she was sailing on Loon Lake. It was never explained other than, "She's just Aunt Mary Cunningham."

I was six or seven years old when she first started the encapsulation exercises that sometimes snuck up on me. Her smell would usually warn me, but if I was preoccupied at Big Daddy's candy counter, or catching a bumble bee (the white faced ones don't sting) around the privet hedges near the store, and didn't see or smell her coming, the shout of "Mr. Boy! Give Aunt Mary Cunningham [*she* even said her whole name] a big old hug!" I was trapped. But being hugged from behind gave me needed breathing room, as opposed to turning suddenly into her rack-of-clothes get-up and getting dangerously lost in all that mothballed and Evening-in-Paris clothes hamper. She was the closest thing to crazy I was exposed to up to that point.

But then she brought her friend and neighbor, Uncle Tom Smith (also always a three named moniker) to our post office one day. He was the oldest black man in Putnam, and because he lived in a kerosene lit house without running water, he smelled of petroleum mixed with tiger cages at the zoo. Even though he scared me to the point of shaking, I was fascinated with what he always had in his inside coat pocket, which he would entice me to come closer to see. "Come here, Mr. Boy, and see's what I's got to show ya!" That got me every time. I have a hard time

47

Our Post Office today

trying to remember anything in his pocket, other than the day he took these tiny glass vials out and said, "Look close, Mr. Boy. Look inside the glass. I's got these out my ears yestiddy!" The three glass vials each had a honeybee in them. Two were dead, drowned in their own bee spit. The other one was dying and struggling to crawl up the slimy glass walls of its coffin. "Can you hear 'em?" he said. "They's been talkin' in my head for a long time. Now's they's out. You want 'em?"

No. No I don't.

I couldn't say it.

Just shook my head as if it was trapped in the middle of a huge bowl of colorless Jello. My head seemed to not want to move to right or left as bad as I wanted it to. The Jello finally melted away and by this time he had placed them back into his inside coat pocket, and gone past me into the post office. I was still standing there when he and Aunt Mary Cunningham came out and passed me on their way to their world of crazy; she the Queen, and he the King of Crazies. The last thing I heard was Uncle Tom Smith, leaning into one of her hats as he reached into his inside coat pocket and whispered, "Do you wants to see what's I's got out of my ear yestiddy?"

48

She reared back her head, held on to both her hats, and let out a laugh that in that moment seemed to travel through time to somewhere out beyond that summer sky in Putnam, Alabama. I'll bet it's still traveling, getting bigger and louder as it flies past stars and moons and eventually invades heaven.

On some days in July, when I watch a honeybee visit my Carolina Jasmine on the back deck, I hear that laugh and wonder if Aunt Mary Cunningham and Uncle Tom Smith were really from Putnam, or if I was the luckiest kid on the planet that summer to be visited by sideshow aliens. Strange smelling aliens that had landed somewhere down by the Tombigbee River, and wandered into town on Saturdays to tease a young human being they simply called … "Mr. Boy."

11

Billy Earl & Mr Shinny:
Made up names for a
true story

Billy Earl was a wild, feral, wolf-boy that lived down the road going towards the Tombigbee River. We were forbidden to play together because he stole at least one of my toys every time he came into our yard. But I looked forward to seeing him, all of a sudden appearing by the pump house or standing down by the barn or behind me, without me knowing he was there. I could tell he was near because of his smell. It was a mixture of soured, sweaty clothes and cigarettes. Billy Earl smoked. He was nine.

I was seven.

He looked like he was 40. There were poor white people in Putnam and then there was his family. I don't remember ever seeing his Daddy, but his Mama sometimes helped my Mama around the house. We didn't have much money, but they had practically nothing.

When he stole my wooden airplane, Mama put me in the car, drove to their house on the river road, and left me in the car while she angrily walked into their dog trot house. Only a few seconds passed before his Mama pulled Billy Earl out into the yard and beat the hell out of him. Mama was standing there with my airplane and all of a sudden his Mama handed Billy Earl over to my Mama and politely held my airplane while my Mama whipped Billy Earl. Seeing him whipped by his Mama was kinda fun, but when my Mama was spanking his skinny ass, something came over me and I started to cry. That poor, smelly wild boy was no better than the yard dogs we all threw things at when they came too near the back porch. I think I fell in love for the first time. Billy Earl was kinda my first pet. And everybody was ganging up on him. He never got to officially come to the house again after the airplane tragedy. But I still loved and missed him. When we did get to see each other again, it was always one of those sudden appearances he was so good at.

My grandfather and grandmother, Big Daddy and Big Mama, owned one of the two general stores in Putnam and behind their store was an old tin roofed house, set off to an angle with a dirt road leading up to it. One of Putnam's many town drunks lived there, with his Mama. Let's just call him Mr. Shinny. Mr. Shinny also had a squirrel monkey that he had ordered from the Spiegel catalog. This was the 1950s, when you could order just about anything from Spiegel. I used to get the catalogs, sit down with a 5¢ Coca-Cola in a bottle, some mayonnaise-and-saltine cracker sandwiches, and be in heaven. Coatimundies from South America (called Snookum-Bears). The "no sex-choice – only $5 monthly" note at the end of the animal's description always bothered me, but I never asked what it meant. Hell, I was shopping from National Geographic! Spiegel's BIG PLUS BUDGET POWER tagline made it seem that I could own any of them. I couldn't of course.

One day, though, Billy Earl snuck up behind me at Big Daddy's store and whispered, "Mr. Shinny's got a monkey!" And then another Billy Earl-gets-Ronald-into-deep-shit episode began. Billy Earl, who didn't think Hell was hot, walked right up to Mr Shinny's door, didn't knock, just yelled, "Mr. Shinny, we wanna see your monkey!" And when Mr. Shinny opened that door and stood there with that little alien thing sitting on his shoulder, jerking his little scared head and screeching, I truly saw God for the first time. All the things I had ever wanted, from a train set to a television (we didn't get one of those until I was in the third grade) just paled beside the vision I saw before me. I had been scared to death of Mr. Shinny, but that day he was merely a perch for the cutest, most desirable thing I had ever seen. I remember the smell coming from Mr. Shinny's mouth: sour mash moonshine whiskey and tobacco, and the words he said. But no fear of the man my Mama had warned me about could stop me now. Once when my sister was crying and Mama asked what was wrong, my sister replied, "That man over there scares me!" To which my Mama replied (I'm still shocked today – my saintly mother) "You have every right to be scared of that son-of-a-bitch."

Oh yes, the words that came from his mouth that day, "Jist don't you let him git away from ya." Little did me and Billy Earl know just what those words meant. The monkey Spiegel had described as "exceptionally small, hardly any larger than a squirrel. Delightful household pet – cheerful, lively, sensitive and affectionate – but not destructive" and "no sex choice – only $5 monthly," didn't prepare me in the least for what was about to happen. Why did Mr. Shinny say "Jist don't let him git away from ya?"

We were about to find out.

The pitiful screeching as Mr. Shinny tore the thing away from his shoulder and handed it to Billy Earl still wakes me up at night. My God, it was like its arms had been ripped out of their sockets. It wailed like we were a hot stove it had jumped on. Mr. Shinny gave me, the little Harris boy who always seemed responsible, the monkey's leash. It was a piece of well rope tied to a ring on the monkey's collar. I was scared shitless, but still thrilled to be near something I wanted so badly but could never have. Daddy had said, "We don't have $32.89 for any squirrel monkey. You have a real squirrel. It was free."

I had the leash. Billy Earl had the screaming monkey and when Mr. Shinny closed the door, Billy Earl threw that little furry alien on the ground and yelled words I had never heard before. I was shocked at Mama's "son-of-a-bitch," but "Damn you, you little monkey fucker" was new to me. I liked the way it sounded. So much so that... I dropped the rope.

The monkey took off like a scalded cat and went up the nearest tree, still screaming bloody murder. Billy Earl was no help. He wouldn't get near the monkey, so I had to climb up the tree to – God knows what – and try to get it to come down. "Don't let it git away from ya" was now a death knell. Mr. Shinny would kill both of us. After all, he was a "mean son-of-a-bitch." I got near the little thing, who was looking at me with its Spiegel "large expressive eyes, black nose spot and tiny white, no sex choice – only $5 monthly" face and I reached toward it. Why? To stroke it? To pinch its tiny white cheeks? No. To grab the little "monkey fucker!"

Well, it knew I had no love, only fear in my eyes so it did what any squirrel monkey with a black nose spot would do; it

53

bit the crap out of my index finger. It hooked onto it and the shock, pain, and panic resulted in my jerking back as hard as I could. The air changed, my world stopped spinning as I looked at the blood squirting out of my completely split finger tip onto the ground several miles below. I was going to die from monkey rabies, and so I did what I was so good at. I fainted and fell out of the tree.

When I woke up, Mama was whipping me, the monkey was gone and so was Billy Earl. How all that occurred, I have no memory of. All I remember was the rag on my finger, the ride home and the white enamel pan with kerosene in it that my Mama stuck my finger in, leaving me sitting there on the back porch. Kerosene kills rabies.

What I most remember, as I watched the blood ooze out of my finger into the kerosene, is how the blood didn't mix with the kerosene, but came out of my wound like a slithering red snake squirming across the white pan bottom from where it had been trapped in my veins just waiting to be released to its freedom by the teeth of a "monkey fucker." Mama took the Spiegel catalog and burned it in the fire barrel behind the house.

Billy Earl came into my life two more times after that: once while running around the shed in our back yard playing hid-and-seek with Junior going lickety-split. There he was, as always, appearing out of nowhere, and I ran smack into him. Billy Earl was made of granite. I bounced off him like a ricocheted BB and passed out in mid-air. The impact knocked the wind out of me, and I didn't even remember hitting the ground just fainted in mid-air. I came to, once again, with Mama whipping me. I guess she saw Billy Earl running down the road and blamed me for playing with him again.

Junior was over by the porch laughing. I didn't speak to him for days. Junior never really understood me. I didn't really understand me. I know my Mama didn't. Billy Earl probably came the closest because he knew I envied his freedom, his mischief, his joie de vivre. His grin said it all. He always knew I loved seeing him. One of my favorite fantasies when I was young, was to imagine seeing a real Indian stepping out from behind a big tree when I would be alone in the woods. Around Thanksgiving especially, when I was roaming over to our south forty, crossing the open broom sage fields and skirting the edge of the woods, I thought I sometimes saw, just disappearing behind a big oak or hickory, the back of a Native American with his quiver blending into the tree. I would stand there waiting for him to emerge on the other side of the tree, but he never did.

Billy Earl was my Indian.

Speaking of war paint, the next and last time I saw Billy Earl was the best. Although I got another whipping for it, it's still my favorite time ever at church and my favorite time ever with Billy Earl.

He and church were not usually used in the same sentence. He never went inside. He couldn't sit down that long. One summer, during a revival, he appeared, this time out of the dark. There was a tradition at Putnam Baptist Church during a revival. The women all went directly into the church when the preacher appeared at the door for starting time, and the men folk all gathered just outside the front of the church to have one last cigarette, or to talk about the weather, crops, or various men things. We boys got to stay outside with them. The women would sing the first hymn, and we got one last chance to run around. The men would finish their cigarette, or snuff, or chewing tobacco and then go into church. They'd spit out the tobacco, wipe with their fingers the snuff out of their bottom lip, or toss the cigarette butts under the front steps. There were no filters in the early 50s, just smoldering butts slowly burning out there on the gravel under the steps. One night, early in the week, Billy Earl appeared as our dads were going up the steps. His timing was perfect. Out of the dark and into my life – again. Other boys and I would tag after our dads, and that night, I caught a glimpse of Billy Earl as he waited out in the gloom. I took a fateful chance and hung back. He scurried under the steps and I looked over the railing to what he was doing. With two or three cigarette butts stuck in his mouth, he was taking turns puffing one, removing it to puff another. I was spellbound. Then someone opened the door, saying, "Son it's time for you to come in," or it may have been my mother, "Ronald, get in here!"

I knew the routine would happen each night, and so I waited. The second night of the revival, Billy Earl came out of the dark as he had the night before and saw me. He motioned, and I joined him under the steps, knowing it was an early trip to Hell if I got caught. He taught me how to inhale. The first intake poured molten lava into my lungs, and I threw the butt down. It seemed to never reach the ground, but somehow levitated to Billy Earl's lips and glowed there with the one already in his mouth. It looked exactly like both the Devil's eyes glowing under the steps of the Putnam Baptist Church.

What came next was totally unexpected. Billy Earl said, "Gimme a nickel." What? "Gimme a nickel!" He knew I had money for our offering, so he had a hare-brained idea to make a little cash. "Gimme a nickel and I'll run into the side of the church with my head!" He knew we loved violence. And so I gave him a nickel. Jesus and the missionaries would just have to wait for my money. I was buying a ticket to Ringling Brothers. I didn't know it at the time (never realizing just how smart Billy Earl really was), but he wasn't actually hitting his head, but smacking his hand against the wall first, to make it look like it was his head smashing the wall. He would moan, stagger back, and hold out his hand for another nickel. He always picked a wall away from the congregation, to attract less attention. Mama and Daddy, and the rest of the congregation, probably looked up from the Broadman Hymnal at the sound and reckoned it to be a dog or a wild hog running loose. I sometimes sat by my second cousin Margaret Singleton in the back, so I guess that's why Mama and Daddy didn't miss me.

As the week wore on, I convinced my folks to give me more nickels to give to Jesus and the missionaries. I was really investing in the transition of Billy Earl to a mushbrain idiot that I could push around like a rope tied sack of shelled corn. When he staggered back from the "impact," I would run up and touch him and he would fall over and I'd shiver all over. Touching the wild boy and causing him to fall down conquered my fear of him. Little did I know, I was the victim – of a scam by Billy Earl to rob Jesus and the missionaries, of his cleverness to get back at a privileged little snothead who secretly wanted him as a ragdoll, and most of all, his plan to keep me out of the church so I would get into the same trouble that he was so used to.

The last night of the revival took the Billy Earl cake. He came out of the woods with a jar of lightning bugs. Perfect timing. No dads in sight as I glanced toward his always grand entrance from behind the big oak tree that anchored the tables used for the annual Dinner-on-the-Ground. He held up the jar like a lighthouse beacon, and I was once again suckered into his untamed world. He opened the jar, grabbed a couple of lightning bugs, took their rear ends between his forefinger and thumb and did the damnest thing. He smeared the lightning bug bottoms across his forehead and there in the dark I saw my first magic trick. The fluorescence streaked across his face like a comet's tail, and as he grabbed more fireflies and turned his face into a neon Indian on the warpath, I was putty in his hands. Grabbing those poor insects, smearing my face in wild abandon and running around in silent joy probably raised my happiness level to its zenith at that point in my life.

But, as the sun always sets, so did my joy. Billy Earl's madness was immeasurable. He coerced me, with little resistance, into climbing up on his shoulders, and looking into the church window at the congregation. Seeing my Mama's face blanche at me looking into God's house while she was singing, "The Old Rugged Cross," suddenly took all the joy of knowing Billy Earl out of my head and heart. As she quickly rose, passed my Daddy sitting there in our pew – the second on the left from the front – I knew Billy Earl was about to vanish from my life. And I was to receive the worst whipping of my life.

He did. And I did.

Mocking God's house was the last straw. It broke more than the camel's back. It burned my butt up so bad that I sat raised up on that pew with my hands pressing into those hard wooden slats until the benediction. I cried silently as she handed me Daddy's handkerchief, which he always had in his back pocket, never saying a word, but I knew – "Wipe that junk off your face and start singing!" I don't remember the song, but I knew I'd never see Billy Earl again. He caused too much pain, even though it was usually worth it. He had done the most magic thing ever. He had painted me to look like my most secret fantasy.

When my Mama had finished whipping me, I saw him at the edge of the church woods, grinning and slipping out of sight. His face was glowing like … like the Indian in my daydream. Like someone who knew your best-kept secret and would rather die than tell anybody. His grin said it all. It always did.

That last time, it was painted in light.

12

This was when I was like nine:
Killing my sister

My youngest sister Lena Carol, and I didn't get along… I hated her. They tell me I was one of the worst children ever raised. No fault of my parents… I had somehow decided that the whole world belonged to me. I also think I was a mistake because there was five years difference between my youngest sister and eight between me and Celia, my oldest sister. So I was just wrong and spoiled and the only boy. But they did things that made me really, really, really mad.

Elvis.

There is no way to describe the middle-to-late 1950s with Elvis. I was in sixth grade when he exploded. The sound. Nobody had heard it before. It was like "Don't Be Cruel" was a weird Jesus advice song, mixed up with drunk hunters shootin' at each other and yelling "You Ain't Nothing But a Hound Dog." Those were two things my life revolved around – the church and animal slaughter. I was hypnotized and knew his music wasn't quite right. And being so bad, I figured he knew something I needed to know.

Now, my sisters had a radio in our room. We all slept in the same room, my sisters in the bed against the wall and me in the one in the middle of the room. My room. But they would close the door when he came on the radio, and lock it to keep me out. So the only way I could listen to Elvis was to go outside and squat down under the window.

One day I was out there and "Don't Be Cruel" was playing, and something happened to me. I had had enough. Only my sister Lena Carol was in there, so I figured I had a chance to kill them one at a time. I got my BB gun, and went to the door of my room, and I called to my sister that I wanted to listen to Elvis. She yelled through the door, "You can't!" and I yelled back "I'm going to shoot you! I've got my BB gun, and I'm gonna shoot you!" She just laughed her cackle and said, "You don't have any BBs. Mama took those away from you." I had killed some birds or something – probably a mockingbird – and she was right, I didn't have any. Well dammit, I was gonna find something. Mama had shelled some little things called lady peas for seeds for next year's crop. They were dry, tiny little things, a little bit bigger than a BB.

And I think this was my first remembered cleverness. I felt empowered as I reached in that bowl, and filled my BB gun with those lady peas. I had forgotten about Elvis and "Don't Be Cruel." I had ammunition and I was going to take my room back. So I went to the room and knocked on the door and bellowed,

Celia, Ronald and Lena Carol

"Let me in!" and she bellowed back "No!" Well I went outside, knowing I had a deadly weapon, and thought, "I'm going to try one more thing before I kill her." So I grabbed a brick that Daddy had laid out under a rain spout and came back in, stood in the foyer in front of the room, and threw the brick as hard as I could at the door. Well, this really pissed off my sister, probably scared her good. I know it scared the crap out of me. Until I left that house ten years ago, there was still a big dent in that door where I had hit it. Even the many paint jobs my Daddy did to the walls didn't completely cover the wrath of my youth.

She opened the door and I cocked that BB gun, aimed it right at her head... and I shot her... because I wanted her to die. Well, I didn't know the peas would work – I didn't know anything other than being pissed. The lady pea/BB hit her right under her left eye, and she fell screaming down to the floor. She was dead, I thought.

Then the whole situation turned 180 degrees. I had killed my sister! I had meant to frighten her, but instead I had killed her with a lady pea. And for the first time in my life I realized that I was probably a little shithead, and that I was going to Hell. Then this great fear came over me, because I knew I was going to be beat to death because I had committed sister-cide.

I ran out of the house, threw the BB gun in the backyard, and ran all the way to the woods in the back of the house. Now, there were two things that scared me when I was young. One, the Boogerman that lived upstairs, and two, the Boogerman that lived in the woods. Not bogey man, or boogie man, but Boogerman. In the South it's a Boogerman! In the daytime there's no Boogerman. So I ran way over beyond the garden, into the woods, and hid behind a tree. This was like 300 feet – a football field – away from the house. And I stayed there for hours, hearing my Mama calling, hearing my Daddy calling, hearing my name listed with those bad children that the Devil was going to send straight to Hell that day. Knowing that when I went home that I would be dismembered and shipped off to the Devil in Tupperware cake plates, and slowly fed to the hounds of Hell. So I stayed in the woods – I was so scared – and I was genuinely sorry. This was the first time I was contrite about anything.

Then it got dark. The choice was to be beaten by my Mama and my Daddy or be eaten alive by the Boogerman. So... I snuck home. I slouched toward Calvary. And got there and rightfully got beaten, I think by everybody in the house. Everybody. I think if Mama had had company she would let them beat me too.

But I learned. I learned. It was the first time that I actually liked my sister. I had to try to kill her to like her. She was alive. I liked her. Things were wonderful, even though I had trouble sitting down for a couple days.

It was just a horrible, horrible lesson. It was my jail term, it was my electric chair, it was my Boogerman – all that. Of course the BB gun was taken away from me, and the only time I used it again was sneaking it and cocking it and forgetting to put the handle back and pulling the trigger. Well you know what happens; the handle snaps back into the slot like a guillotine, and SMACK, down on your guilty fingers and breaks all of them – or so I thought. It's so painful you crumble to the ground with the gun still gripping and smashing you. The pain flooding all over you. You feeling sick and faint and hurt and punished and it was all because I was not supposed to touch that BB gun.

So, those two things: the killing of my sister, and the cocking of the handle of the off-limits-attempted-murder-weapon probably turned me into... a civilized boy.

My Pee-pee: Bruised by bicycles

*M*ichael Young had a new bicycle. One that had tassels hanging from the handle bar grips. One that had a bell. One that had a rocket shaped head light. One that had everything mine didn't. One that I worshipped.

We often went riding down the dirt road at the south end of their big yard that ended up at a place called Blue Rock on the Tombigbee River. We never went that far because of a long, steep hill that we could never have made back up. Except one day.

That rainy summer had made a single set of deep logging truck ruts on the hill and there was no passing of vehicles, so one truck waited at the bottom if it met another or waited at the top. The ruts were about a foot deep, and straight as an arrow. A bicycle going down that hill in one of those ruts would pick up enough speed to lift you into a solo flight for at least a mile. That's what summer vacation does to a boy's imagination. Freedom in the country had nothing to do with logic; we were capable of flying if we could pick up enough speed.

Michael dared me. I took off. I picked up much more speed than I anticipated and much sooner than I expected. About half way down the hill as my legs were spread out to the kudzu flying past on both sides of the road, the axis of the earth shifted imperceptibly, and my bike and I started to angle slightly to the right. Caught in the narrow tire rut I had no leverage to upright myself. Although I was flying lickety-split through July gum-filled air with the sweet smell of kudzu flowers making my flight euphoric, I knew I was going to die.

Because of the acceleration and the narrow rut, the bike and I leaned further and further to the right, and I began to imagine the layers of boy flesh being peeled away from my bones as my bullet body, slowly making contact with the hard, jagged Alabama clay, slid like a pine log into the buzz saw of a planer mill. I swear I rode for hours parallel to the ground as

65

my ten-year-old life flashed before me. A lot of it seemed to be tinted a sick color of orange. Maybe I was staring into the sun and burning my retinas, or maybe my stomach contents were entering my eyeballs.

I was sure in my soon to-be-puréed brain, Michael would ride his bike back to his mother and tell her about my lying in the kudzu dying, and they would rush me to the hospital in Butler and Dr. Clark would shoot me up with morphine to ease my last gasping pain-ridden breaths. And then the ground found me. The bike stopped. I didn't. The handle bar grip, dug into my groin as I went flying towards the tangled lost world of deceptive kudzu. The pain of the impact into my "down there" was so intense I of course passed out. The last thing I remember was how much like a Grapico drink the kudzu flowers smelled. Grapico was what Mama used for the "blood" of Jesus for communion. At least I was certain to die and go to heaven. Smell is important when you are dying.

I don't know how long I was out, but it was getting dark when I came to. I managed to sit up, but the pain laid me back down. I knew the gripless handlebar had cut my pee-pee off, and I couldn't even look down there. I just lay there and stared at the dying of the light. What I didn't know was that Michael had gotten back to his house, gotten distracted (he had every toy imaginable,) and forgotten to tell his mother about my death. Later that afternoon she noticed my absence, "Where's Ronald?" she asked. Michael said nonchalantly, 'Oh I forgot, he wrecked his bike at the bottom of the hill going to the river.'"

She flew down to my Mama's house, got her and the three of them went to view my corpse. I was sitting up now and crying of course. But the pain was easing. I still hurt like hell, but there was so much care getting me comfortable in the car that I was feeling much better. Daddy came the next day with his pick-up and got my bike. It was all bent up, but he could fix anything. I thought Mama would fuss at me for being so stupid. But she said nothing for the days I healed. Then one day after I was back to normal, out of the blue, she told me to go to the privet hedge in the back yard and get a switch. I was puzzled. Who was it for? I hoped one of my sisters had been bad. They never got whipped. I was glad to oblige. I got the switch. A big one. Gave it to her and, there on our back porch, she beat the hell out of my legs. She never said a word, but I knew through my tears that even though she was thankful I had not died on the river road, she was making sure I didn't do anymore stupid bicycle tricks.

I never told her that Junior was riding his bike one day, and I was sitting behind him on the little seat and he hit a bump. I bounced onto the back tire because he had no fender over his back wheel. My pee-pee was propelled by the tire into the metal fork that held the wheel. As I screamed for him to stop because the wheel was grinding my monkey into sausage, he kept saying, "Don't tell your Mama! Don't tell your Mama!" He knew we would both be beaten within an inch of our lives. I limped around for days with the sorest tally whacker ever, but when around Mama I walked upright-and in great pain. I knew death might be an option if she found out, and I had not learned my lesson about bicycles, so I avoided her as much as possible.

I mentioned orange earlier, but there are no colors to describe the stages of a severely bruised pee-pee going through the healing process. Aubergine: deep reddish purple brown; cordovan: burgundy and dark rose; chartreuse: halfway between green and yellow are three that come close. Too close.

The hot pepper Pee-pee story

May is my favorite month: my birthday (the 23rd,) end of school, and May Day. I was in the third grade and Margaret Singleton and I were elected to be Sun Bonnet Sally and Overall Jim respectively, though I would have been either. (The idea of wearing a bonnet fell in line with the thrill of the green Dotted Swiss recital dress; both together would have been Christmas!) In any event, we had been selected for the May Day Celebration. Sun Bonnet Sally and Overall Jim were kinda the first warm ups to being May Day King and Queen. That happened in the fifth grade. We were on track with the certainty of being elected if we had already fulfilled the junior roles of Sun Bonnet Sally and Overall Jim.

Sunbonnet Sally & Overall Jim

We were May Day Prince and Princess the next year on our way to King and Queen, but Margaret lost out to June Pope for Queen because, I suspect, it had something to do with me smacking Margaret's forehead one day on the playground by slinging the swing and nailing her cranium. I was in love with June Pope. Margaret was my second cousin, and there was a limit on grammar school love with your cousin, especially if you knocked her noggin in about an inch or two. Jerry Vice, my best friend, and I loved June Pope so much we learned to play the triangle and drums (two very complicated syncopation instruments) in the Sweet Water Grammar School Rhythm Band. We chose these two instruments, (me, the triangle, and Jerry, the drum.) just to be on either side of her. She could play a recorder beautifully. She was perfect. We were in love with her for three years, and then I was voted May Day King to her May Day Queen. Jerry sought revenge.

There is no wrath like a love sick twelve-year-old boy scorned. It was on Halloween that next fall. The sixth grade. I was at the Halloween Carnival that was held annually in

Prince and Princess of May day

the gym. It was at the Home Canned Foods Booth that he got me. All kinds of home canned foods were on display for sale, and each food would either have a picture of a fruit or vegetable or the actual produce would be in a bowl or basket beside the jars. I didn't know about hot peppers. I knew Mama sometimes made Hot Pepper Sauce, but we didn't grow them. She got them from neighbors. There they were, piled in a bowl all shiny and green and shaped like our cocker spaniel's wee-wee. Jerry knew about hot peppers and he knew about wee-wees. We had never shown each other our "privates," but he said if we took some of the hot peppers and went to the bathroom and rubbed them on our pee-pees (wee-wees were for dogs) then they would get bigger and bigger. I had experienced erections before, but didn't know what to do with them or why they happened.

The idea of intentionally making my thing bigger fascinated me. He was still mad at me about the June Pope thing, but I had foolishly forgotten about that over the summer. I thought he was still my best friend. We went to the bathroom. He said go first. So I grabbed the hot pepper like he said, broke it in half like he said, and pulled down my pants. There it was, quiet and small. But the magic pepper would change all that he said. I excitedly rubbed the broken hot pepper all over my "Pee-pee" and in a nanosecond saw his grin and knew. He still loved June Pope and still hated me.

The brush fire traveled up my jerking body, turned into a five alarm forest fire that burned through my innards and came out of my eyes like red hot pokers and traveled back to my down there and branded "stupid" on my melted monkey. He laughed himself down into the floor and I started crying. My pee-pee hurt so bad I wanted to die.

For some reason, Jerry took pity on my wanting to die and told me to sit backwards on the commode, facing the tank, and splash water on it and it would put out the fire. I splashed and splashed and splashed. The burning kind of stopped, but I had no normal feeling in that whole area, like when your foot goes to sleep or right after you get a tooth filled. I wondered how I would know when I had to pee due to the numbness. I was just thankful it hadn't burned up and fallen off. Jerry told me he was sorry, but he still grinned for no apparent reason every now and then. I would look at him and he would stop, but he knew I'd never tell anyone what he did because boys don't pull down their pants in front of each other if they still want to get chosen for softball at P.E. June Pope and her mother moved away at the end of that year, but Jerry and I stayed best friends all the way through high school.

Me and Jerry

There never was another June Pope and there didn't have to be. She was always between us playing her shiny black recorder and as we glanced out the corner of our eye, we could still see her in profile. Just beyond that profile we also saw each other and our solid friendship.

I have a framed picture of Jerry and me in my house. It's May Day and we're both eating ice cream cones. It's the Spring after that Halloween. We're both grinning. We both know why.

15

The squirrel stories

I don't have any pets now. When I was young, I was severely traumatized by two pets I had that died. I loved them more than I loved my sisters. It was close to an unnatural thing. But at the time, it occupied my days. I woke up to be with my friends. A squirrel named – of course – Nutty and a parakeet named Dickey Bird. My mother and father tolerated the obsession, I think, just to keep me from doing damage to such things as my toys or my sisters. Or maybe just to keep me from dressing up in my sisters' recital dresses and dancing in the back yard.

My father was a squirrel and deer hunter and he was a

wonderful shot. And squirrel meat was needed. It wasn't like a sport. Much more of a hunter-gatherer thing. He would go down to the swamp somewhere near the Tombigbee River to a place called Barney's Upper or Barney's Lower. The Barneys had been a landed gentry family owning half the world that I knew – raising cotton and corn during the late 1800s and early 1900s. When Daddy hunted there it was a privileged thing for having done some good deed or some legal paper work for the local wealthy that now owned the hunting rights. He always came home with his mustard-colored hunting coat filled with dead squirrels, stuffing the inside pockets that lined the bottom rim with blood stains seeping on the outside because the rubber lining had worn thin. It was horrific to me. Absolutely horrific. If you put your hand in there to get the trophies, they sometimes were still warm, or they were stiff, cold, lumps like quarter-moon shaped bodies in bloody rigor-mortis.

But one time he brought me a baby squirrel. He had shot the rest and killed the Mama that fell out of the tree, and a baby squirrel fell with her. He had the biggest heart of any killer in Marengo County, so I got my first pet. It was just beyond pink, that stage where you see the blue veins through the hairless pinkish skin. Its eyes were still shut, glued together by baby stuff that finally is licked away by the Mama squirrel. I pulled gently at its eyes every day thinking it would be blind all its life if I didn't. My sisters had doll bottles, so I got Mama to put fresh cow's milk in them as I sat in the foyer of our house and nursed it. I wanted a place it could grow up and this was the smallest room in the house. You could close all the doors leading into the foyer from the bathroom, living room, our bedroom, Mama and Daddy's room, and the folding doors to upstairs. It cried like a baby does until I fed it. It was my doll, my child, my own. Nobody I knew had a squirrel. The day it opened its eyes and saw me, made me the happiest little boy in Putnam. There were

Nutty

only seven little white boys close to my age in Putnam: me and Jesse Little, Max Johnson, Mike and Pat Young, John Singleton and of course, Billy Earl, but remember Billy Earl was raised by wolves and Mama wouldn't let him play with me. Bad influence.

Anyway Nutty thought I was his Mama. He would cry until I held him. I guess he was a "him." I didn't know anything about squirrel pee-pee's or squirrel nuts. I didn't know I had nuts. I thought for a long time they were cancers. Things I got for being bad. I prayed they would go away. I didn't dare touch them. Lumps that had no purpose. Growths that I heard my Mama and Daddy talk about being on people like goiters or wens or tumors. I certainly didn't connect me being a boy with Nutty being a boy squirrel; I just knew I had a baby!

I recently read about squirrel rescuers in New York City called "rehabbers," who take care of abandoned baby squirrels and when they are little like Nutty was, they – are you ready for this? – have to stimulate their genitals with a wet Q-tip to get them to urinate or defecate. I'm glad I never read a "How to Raise a Baby Squirrel" book. Mama would have frowned on the Q-tip thing. A six-year old boy swabbing a baby squirrel's privates – not Christian!

When Nutty got older Daddy built him a little tree house on the lowest limb of the big pecan tree in the back yard. He slept out there and stayed loyal to me. Mama didn't really like "it" in the house, but she tolerated me. I got this weird feeling one day that Nutty wanted a friend, because he was an enemy to the feral dogs and cats that kinda hung out at our house. We went to Selma to see our doctors, and on one trip I saw parakeets for the first time in my life. We didn't get National Geographic. Too many African breasts and Masai monkey things hanging down. I saw them in the library at school and all that really scared me. I though they were deformed. Anyway, my folks bought me a green parakeet, and I named it Dickey Bird. It was for Nutty. And they fell in love. They would scamper across the back of the couch, stop and chatter, and then take off. Up the strings of the Venetian blinds like lianas in an Amazon jungle. Nutty would meet Dickey Bird on the curtain valance, and they would talk squirrel/bird talk and take off. They were my television, my View Master, my journeys to exotic lands. I couldn't wait to get home from elementary school in the afternoons and let them play. Mama kept them caged all day. Bird or squirrel dooky in her house was ungodly!

Then Christmas came. Both of them somehow made their way to the kitchen where they never had been before, but in all the hubbub and people here and there, they somehow got in there. Dickey Bird flew up onto the cabinet door by the sink and Nutty just naturally got up there by climbing the strings up the blinds at the table window. Before I could get in there, I could hear Mama yelling to get the bird and squirrel out of her kitchen. Now her kitchen at Christmas time was the best smelling place on earth. Oranges and apples were cut up for ambrosia, her apple sauce cake was just out of the oven. Whiskey on the fruits cakes, the greasy animal fat smell of baked turkey coming from under tin foil, pecan and lemon ice box pies cooling on the Formica topped table. Oh my God – heaven! Mama thought a wild bird flying into the house was bad luck, so Dickey Bird and Nutty together in her kitchen, on Christmas – get 'em out!

Before I could get to them, Dickey Bird flew across the kitchen to the valance over the frosted glass in the back door. Nutty, giddy from the chase and drunk on the smells of Christmas Day took off after Dickey Bird. He made it only half way. Fell on the ceramic divider of our huge kitchen sink and instantly broke his back. Mama, never looking at me, because she was too busy, said simply, "Son, get the squirrel out of my sink." When I picked it up I knew. It folded in my hand like a furry rag and whimpered and… died. Mama heard its cry and calmly gave me the dish towel from her shoulder to wrap him in. I didn't cry. I was in shock. Only after I lay down with him in front of the heater in the living room across the room from the Christmas tree and all of Jesus' birthday presents, did I fall apart and let my broken heart bleed. The towel had an embroidered squash on it and there was no blood. That yellow squash, my grey-brown friend with closed eyes. I thought of the first day I got him.

I lay there all day and finally after all the presents had been opened by relatives – they allowed me to be sad, they never said anything to me – my Daddy and I buried Nutty in the back yard under his house in the pecan tree. We made a little wooden cross out of tomato stakes and I hung a little red Christmas ball on the place where the stakes meet. I don't remember what I got from Santa Claus or from relatives or from Mama and Daddy that Christmas. I think Baby Jesus was probably sad that particular birthday. I still have the Baby Jesus from our Christmas crèche.

I keep it in my car. Only writing this story made it clear to me why I drive with it. Baby Jesus is my surrogate pet. Birth and death. Same day. No more pets for me – ever.

Dickey Bird died two days later when it flew into the grease pot Mama kept on the stove from bacon drippings. She reacted in the same tone she did when Nutty died, "Son, get the bird out of the grease pot on my stove." I think Dickey Bird committed suicide from loneliness. I was still too broken-hearted over Nutty to cry. I don't even remember if we buried him. I'm sure we did. Mama kept empty kitchen matchboxes in a cabinet near the stove. She kept everything. So me and Daddy probably buried Dickey Bird in one of those boxes next to Nutty. Some things are too sad to remember.

Many years passed. My Daddy had a 410 shotgun leaning against the wall in a corner of his closet. He installed a sink in there to wash off the day's dirt. It was his space. That shotgun haunted me. I knew one day he would teach me to use it. To hunt squirrels. And sure enough, the day came. He had tried to make it as painless as possible because of Nutty, by teaching me to shoot rats in the barn at night with the 22 rifle. And that was fun. I'd hold the flashlight and follow the rats as they ran on the cross studs that the wallboards were nailed to. He was a dead shot. Never missed. And he taught me how to aim just ahead of a running rat to get it, as he held the light. Most of the time they stopped and stared at the light. Stupid, ugly, stinking, fat rats. I loved killing them. Holding one up by their scaly grey tails as blood dripped out of their mouths and onto the barn floor was the grown-uppest thing I'd ever done. Daddy was proud. Then one day he brought me his hunting coat, handed it to me and said, "Son, there's a family of squirrels in that big oak tree down by the branch. I saw them there the other day." He then went to his closet and got the 410. He got a box of shotgun shells and gave me six shells. He said he had counted six squirrels. I knew he never wasted a shot.

My day in hell began. I put on the coat, took the gun, put the shells in the coat's outside pocket in those rows of woven shell loops, one at the top of each pocket, and started out across the pasture, past the pond, and into the woods where I played with my friend, Junior. Today would change the woods for me forever. I found the tree and lay down on my back looking up at the tree. Put the gun by my side and waited. Then I began to cry. I could hear crows calling. I don't know why I remember there were crows. Even today, they sound like they're warning of danger. And the woods in squirrel season were dank and smelled of mushrooms and rabbit tobacco, a pungent grey-colored plant with brown under leaves supposedly smoke by Indians. I kept crying. And looking up, I saw the family of squirrels. They all looked like Nutty. I watched them for a long time and knew what Daddy expected of me. I put the first shell in and slowly aimed it upward. I was still lying down.

One squirrel separated out from the others and I shot it. It fell near me. I didn't even pick it up. The other squirrels hid and I waited. And cried. After a long time, they came back out and one moved to a branch above me. It was a long day of killing six squirrels. One shell, one squirrel. They all fell around me like bloody fruit. When the last one fell, I collected them with closed eyes, stuffed them into the inside rubber-lined pocket of the hunting jacket and headed home. By then, I had no more tears. I was numb. But you know, in a strange way, I was released. Released from never having to hunt again. Six shells, six shots. Six dead squirrels. A story my Daddy proudly told and told often. We ate the squirrel's, fried with grits and biscuits and homemade peach preserves. Mama even fried the squirrels tongues. Little gristly pieces of muscle, like a tiny chicken's gizzard, placed on a saucer. If my sisters or me had been really good that week, we would get more than one as a reward, a prize, a ritual for pleasing our parents. Mama handed me the saucer. They were all mine.

I never wore the coat or picked up the 410 again. I didn't have to.

But his coat still hangs in my front room closet.

16

My Baptism & Margaret

Margaret Singleton was my second cousin and my best girl friend. Not girlfriend. Just girl friend. The second cousin stuff made it ok if we really "liked" each other, but still we were only ten or eleven. What did we know of romance? Or care.

She found out that Jesus was her savior one night during a summer revival, and since she was so happy about that, I decided the next night to be "saved." It was a "friend thing" that seemed perfectly ok with me and her and Jesus. So at the end of the service, we stood in line together and the whole church came up and shook our hands. A few ladies cried. I never understood the fuss. We would get to go swimming in the creek after we

Margaret

were baptized. How perfect would that be! Horse Creek was our swimming hole. It was also as sacred as the waters of Galilee that John the Baptist dunked Jesus in. I probably expected a white dove to descend onto mine and Margaret's shoulders just after the nose-pinching emergence. I was that caught up in the New Testament. It was better than a Nancy Drew mystery: "The Secret of the Two Fishes," "The Case of the Mad Pigs Running Into the Sea," "The Rolled Away Stone Mystery." Why I never read The Hardy Boys was not an issue. Margaret reminded me of Nancy Drew. I reminded me of Nancy Drew.

After we were baptized, I immediately started swimming. That was short lived. My Mama's voice, yelling at me from the bank of the creek, "Ronald, stop swimming!" was the first time I realized how serious being baptized was. Up until then, it was an excuse to get to go to the creek. Now, after that reprimand that stopped even the mosquitoes from biting, that even turned the heads of a couple of kingfishers perched high above my Mama, I was suddenly changed. My Mama's voice was as powerful as God's descending dove. Since that day, my beliefs were always tinged with guilt, and a touch of shame.

Southern religion defined to the T.

17

Night funeral:
Mr Bennie Moncrieff

I had a rabbit's foot key chain when I started to drive. "For luck," they always said. I looked it up and found the real truth.

"For luck: the left hind foot of a graveyard rabbit killed in the dark of the moon." That's what the book said, and that's what hung from the ignition of my sister's 1955 Chevy. I learned to drive, but the rabbit's foot meant something more to me than my family ever knew. Children and grown-ups are all wary of cemeteries. But cemeteries at night?

I was in the Putnam graveyard one night in "the dark of the moon." Fact is, there was no moon. It was pouring down rain, and I was in the back seat of that same car I learned to drive in.

It was a funeral, a funeral at night, with a circle of cars, their headlights on, all pointing toward the six foot hole in the ground that was slowly filling up with water. Buckets were let down into the grave and a chain of men emptied them as far away from the grave as possible. There was no time for solace or quietude. The body had to be buried quickly or the grave would flood or the batteries would go dead on the cars. There was a ragged circle of umbrellas that hid the faces of everyone in black. The car lights blinded the mourners. I cried out of fear, not sympathy, at this melting picture of death, seen through the front windshield of our car.

"Son, stay in the car. There's no need for you to get wet. He would respect you just by you being here," my Mama or Daddy said. Who said what was all a blur.

"He" was Mr. Bennie Moncrieff, an old hermit bachelor who, whenever I

Putnam cenetary today

saw him, scared me so much I would feel faint. He spoke to me once. I was alone at my house one day when I was seven or eight. I heard a knock on the back wall of the house. I opened the kitchen door and there half-round the corner he stood. He had a bushel basket of turnips. His head was down and his ragged straw hat hid most of his face. He said, "These is for ya Mama." He put them on the porch and, never looking at me, left. I couldn't move. He had been within ten feet of me, and I had this awful feeling that if the screen door had not separated us, he would have come up on the porch and, carried me off to his house in the woods, kept me in his woodshed, and starved me until I was just like the dog skeleton me and Daddy had come across down by the branch behind the house.

"Son, did you thank him?" Mama asked after she found me still standing at the door when she came from the post office. I couldn't talk. I started to cry. She told me something about his life, but nothing registered. He would eventually steal me, was all I could imagine. I never saw him again. Even driving by the dirt road to his house on our way to my grandmother's house made me short of breath. I thought he was sent by the Devil to find me and punish me for all I had done wrong, not minding Mama or Daddy, hating my sisters, burning my toy cars, not praying hard enough in church, or just not praying.

The night funeral proved what I had expected. He was a bad, bad man and could only be buried at night. Quickly, secretly. I didn't know 'til later, or probably didn't hear when it was explained to me by Daddy, that because he had died suddenly, his brothers who lived in Mobile, about 120 miles away, couldn't get off work. So they drove to Putnam after work and drove back that night. Grown-up stuff was still a long way from my understanding. I was watching strangers around my Mama and Daddy bury the man who wanted to steal and starve me. That's all I knew at the time.

On the way back to the house, my Daddy and Mama, both soaking wet, never said a word. Their minds were somewhere lost in sadness that I mistakenly read as silence about something you were not to speak about. About something too dark to ever mention again. It was years later that I heard the truth, or heard it for the second time. A door opened into that shut away night, and Mr. Bennie Moncrieff lifted up out of that smeared snapshot of childhood fear and became just a good neighbor bringing turnips for no good reason other than kindness.

The year he died was 1955. I was ten, and the car I learned to drive in five years later was a 1955. The rabbit foot's dangling there taught me about irony and death, but most of all it taught me about tolerance for those not as lucky as I was. That no one is better than anyone else, just that some of us have had better. I kept the rabbit foot for a long time.

You don't see them much anymore.

Circumcision at twelve

Dr. Clark removed the hood from my bishop when I was 12. It happened in the Choctaw County Hospital in Butler, Alabama. The Random House Dictionary (Concise Edition) says circumcise is "to remove the prepuce of (a male), esp. as a religious rite." What it doesn't say is when the unkindest cut is supposed to happen. The civilized world knows this is done at birth or at the latest, eight days after, according to Jewish custom. Something about the coagulates in the baby boy's blood, like vitamin K, don't form until the eighth day. The eighth day, not the twelfth year.

The prepuce, the hood, the foreskin, whatever you want to label this "stay or go" piece of flesh was mine for enough years for me to have ownership. Religious rites had expired. But one day I was told by my mother that I needed to be "cleaner." That's all she said, "Cleaner."

They took me to the hospital. I went into a small operating room and lay down. A mask was put over my face and when the ether, yes, it was 1957, entered the mask, I floated away into a world where my head felt like there was an entire bale of cotton pushing my brain into the next room. But I was going to be cleaner, so I accepted the being put to sleep as an extra thrill.

This was ether which the Random House Dictionary (Concise Edition) says is 1. A solvent and 2. An inhalant anesthetic or 3. The upper regions of space. The latter is where I was. Space filled with a bale of cotton.

And then I woke up, came to, or came out of it. I knew immediately something really bad had happened to me. I vomited straight up and the contraction of my body, as the puke went everywhere, let me know something in my "down there" was horribly wrong. I don't remember anybody there with me. No nurse, no doctor or family. I'm sure there was, but with the nausea and the cotton brain and the pain, I had an out of body experience because I wasn't prepared for the removal of my monkey. That's what Billy Earl called it; and he was so worldwise I didn't argue with his patois. I knew pee-pee, pecker and monkey. "Spanking" would be added somewhere around the 11th grade.

Anyway, mine was gone. Or so I thought. I wasn't told about prepuce, just cleanliness. It was, "next to Godliness" in our house. The pain was so intense and the bandage so bloody, that my first thought was that 1. I had been such a horrible son, 2. I was doomed to Hell for not loving my sisters, and 3. I was a big disappointment to Jesus, so they had cut off my entire monkey.

Ether is next to truth serum mixed with a little vial of guilt and stirred with a diviner's stick. Pharmaceutical juju. I knew of John the Baptist's head on a platter, but that had to do with somebody dancing and being spoiled rotten. I hadn't learned how to dance yet. But I knew I was spoiled rotten. My reasoning was muddled to say the least. And the pain... I promised God I'd really be a missionary this time if I could just get the doctor to give me back my monkey. I knew I had made a similar promise if I didn't have to testify in front of "The Knife Man." (That episode's in the next story!) I had backslidden on that promise. This time more was at stake. That other promise was about death; this one was about living with no monkey.

I was given massive opiates that week, I think so I wouldn't ask questions as much as for the pain. Nothing was ever discussed. My shame of having been bad and the extreme measure of teaching me a lesson blended into acceptance later on of "looking like the other boys" and "quicker" hygiene.

Somewhere around the second or third day when I had the courage to glance "down there" in my opiate haze, I saw Mr. Monkey was wounded but not dead. I thanked all the versions of God

Mr. Boy at 12

up to that point in my religious upbringing that the removal of the prepuce took place during summer vacation. My parents at least spared me the "show and tell" time at school.

In elementary school I belonged to a club called "The Never-Guess-Look-It-Up Club." We would have five words, one a day, to look up on Friday. It was vocabulary socializing. We elected officers and had a motto: "To make the best better." I was president that next year after the "Death of Mr. Monkey" summer. At the end of the first week of school my list was: ether, missionary, Jewish, pharmacist and antiseptic. I saved "antiseptic" for last and as I wrote it on the board I listed two meanings: 1. free from germs, and 2. exceptionally clean. I underlined clean. Mrs. Pope, my sixth grade teacher probably thought I wanted to grow up to be a doctor or a Baptist nurse in the Holy Land.

The Pontiac & the knife man

*U*p the road from where we lived, about half a mile, lived the Youngs and the Burges, the comfortable, middle class and the not so fortunate, respectively. The Youngs had a maid and the Burges had a pig. The pig came and went as he pleased in their open to the world, small, clapboard house, catty-cornered from the Youngs. Ida Mae Burge was a great "canning" friend to my mother, and they exchanged garden produce like a one-on-one farmers market. The pig was like a dog in the house. No big deal. I would go with my mother to swap out tomatoes, purple hull peas or plum jelly, and the pig would always be in the kitchen. I wanted one so bad, but my mother explained that we had steps coming up to our back porch and the Burges did not. I accepted that only because it was my mother's answer. I knew pigs could climb steps, but my mother's intonations about "steps" told me that no pig would live in my world. We had only one pet that ever came in the house, Ruffles the Cocker Spaniel. He came in only if a door was left open or bad weather came up. When the latter happened, he was immediately removed to the porch because my mother thought dogs attracted lightning. But a pig in the house would probably bring Beelzebub himself, during a summer thunderstorm. She didn't tempt fate. She didn't consider the Devil a welcome guest. In fact, she wouldn't let a wild bird or a "bad news" bee (they were black and yellow with a black head, not yellow and black with a yellow head; those were "good news" bees and allowed to remain) stay in the house for any length of time. Both were bad luck. Bees sting, I got that. A wild bird? Dirty and annoying, I suppose. Oh, and no hats on the bed. Go figure that one! A pig? Nasty and bad luck.

Ida Mae's pig was the cutest, cleanest, sweetest animal I had ever seen. It would look up at you and smile. I swear to God. When I saw the movie *Babe* I didn't marvel at its human features. I had seen Ida Mae's pig and knew they were capable of unconditional love. Reading *Charlotte's Web* was non-fiction to me. I had already been in love with "Some Pig."

Across the road, catty-cornered, the Young children Pat, Michael and Beth were like doll children to me. I was older and they were perfect, life size, amiable and dressed like the children in the Spiegel catalogue. When I went to play with them I felt like a camp counselor arranging their activities because they had every toy, game, bicycle, and sports stuff you could imagine. It was day camp with the Rockefeller kids. So deciding whether to spend a Saturday or an ordinary summer day with Ida Mae's pig or with the Young children was like choosing Christmas over my birthday. Both were perfect. Until one day.

I had walked the road past the gravel pit to the left and the apple orchard on the right, stopped in to say "Hello" to Ida Mae's pig and gone across the road to play with Pat, Michael and Beth. Mrs. Young had a sun porch, a kind of screened in, wicker furniture haven. But today was nice, so we four were in the front yard with balls and bats and general open yard, soft grass, roll around, pretend baseball "camp activities." And then we heard the scream.

It came from the southeast corner of the Young's yard. When I turned toward the scream I saw the Young's maid jump their chain link fence and render this cry-scream. Then we saw why. Across the fence, just behind her was the blur of a man with the sun glinting off the blade of the biggest kitchen knife this side of a machete. I think it was her husband, but to this day I never knew or asked. The only time I had seen a knife this big was to split open a deer after my Daddy had hung it in the backyard after a hunt. The Young's yard was huge, so in the time it took for these two flying figures to reach the front porch where their maid was headed for sanctuary, I looked around for a place for us to hide. I yelled, "Get in the car!" We yanked open the back doors and piled in the back seat. Fifties Pontiacs were land yachts. Kids on trips in those things had enough room to establish territory and never touch each other or fight over a toy. There was so much naugahyde or plush fabric that it was an entire padded cell with corners to claim like kiddie real estate.

I locked all the doors. Those mushroom capped knobs were as prominent as the door handles. They made a loud click as they retreated into the door. Detroit gave you the sound of safety as a bonus for buying all that metal and chrome. That day, at that time, those four clicks were louder than I had ever heard them. A Pontiac had more muscle in every way than our '55 Chevy and, thank God, more room to hide.

When we got the courage to look over the sill of the back window, (it was that big!) the two had reached the porch. The windows of the car were already rolled up because of summer afternoon showers "out of nowhere." The Youngs had big pecan trees in their yard so at least we were not in an oven. Not yet. I was only conscious of dying, stabbed by the deer splitting blade if he saw us. I didn't even consider the heat factor.

Their maid did one of the most amazing things I've ever seen a person do. She grabbed the handle of the screen door, and with certain death at her back, she ripped the entire screen door off its hinges and it tumbled off the porch. By this time Mrs. Young had heard the screams and opened the front door. As their maid collapsed inside, there was a freeze frame moment. Mrs. Young stood in the door frame and as the man with the knife flew up the steps, he seemed to hit an invisible wall. The sight of her defending her home, weaponless, and the sudden realization of his madness washed over him like ice water. He stopped as quickly as a head on collision. We ducked down as she scanned the front yard for us. I was so scared by now that all I could think of was to get as far down into the floorboard as possible. I wanted to get under the carpet. I don't remember even being concerned about Pat, Michael and Beth. I just felt the knife opening me up as I hung upside down from the pecan tree we were under. And then I realized how hot it was in the car. Baked or sliced? So I snuck a peek. He was still standing there facing the closed door, knife hanging at his side. I was beginning to get sick, like throw-up sick, when I heard a squealing of tires, and Mr. Young came barreling into the yard in his pick-up. He probably had been at his mother's, who lived about a small corn field away when Mrs. Young had called him. I don't even think he completely stopped the pick-up, just jumped out, and reached down as he ran, grabbed one of the boys' baseball bats and flew up on the porch. In what seemed like another clock stopping moment, he swung as hard as he could for the man's head. Even with the windows up, the thud was so loud Michael, Pat and Beth peeped over the window sill to see where it came from. The Knife Man collapsed in a heap of overalls, blood and shame. I later found out that he worked for Mr. Young.

What happened after that is a blur. I know we scrambled out of the Pontiac and ran around to the back porch. Mrs. Young called my mother, and she and Daddy came to get me. Not much talk I remember. Just hustling along, getting in our car and going home. As we pulled out into the road and headed home we had to pass that long yard and the corner where the chase began. The Knife Man was still in a clump on the porch as we drove out of sight. I thought he was dead. I was so glad I'd never see him again. I was wrong.

That Fall I was in the fifth grade, 10 or 11 years old, and had already blocked the nightmare out of my summer. It was never mentioned at our house, but I didn't go back to the Young's for the rest of the summer. I still thought The Knife Man had died and everyone was in some kind of silence that always follows a bizarre incident in our home town, a kind of air of denial that it never happened.

And then one day my parents came to school and checked me out. They said we were going to Linden to the court house. My Daddy told me why. He explained that they needed me to be brave and not be afraid. I thought at first that I had been so bad I had to go to jail or that I was adopted and my real parents wanted me back. It was much worse. Now I knew why my Mama had bought me a new outfit and I was wearing it. The Knife Man was not dead and was going to be put on trial. Since Michael, Pat and Beth were too young, I was the only witness. I was going to sit by the judge and he was going to ask me if the man standing in front of me was The Knife Man. The floorboard of the car melted and I turned into boy pudding, slowly dripping onto the road flying below the floorless car. I passed out. The next thing I remember was sitting between Mama and Daddy on a dark oiled bench in a cold room that smelled of cigars and evil. I could hardly see over the bench in front, but I saw a man sitting up high with a black robe on. Mama leaned over and said that was Judge Hasty and a friend of theirs. I didn't care. I was going to die. The Knife Man was going to lunge at me with his knife hidden in his shoe and slice me open before

4th grade

anyone could stop him. I was shaking so hard people were turning to see where the noise was coming from. It was my soul banging up against the back of the bench we were sitting on. Both Mama and Daddy held my hands. I was deer meat wrapped in white butcher paper and stacked in a freezer somewhere in an abandoned house down by the river.

And then The Knife Man came into the courtroom. Two bigger men were on both sides of him. There was a clanging sound as he walked. I closed my eyes and prayed harder than I had ever prayed. This time I meant it. If God would save me from being murdered in front of my parents, Judge Hasty, and most of Marengo County, then I would grow up to be a missionary in some malaria ridden country, be eternally thankful, never fight with my sisters again, and I would rededicate my life to Jesus and this time mean it for more than a few days.

Just before I died I told Mama and Daddy I loved them and waited for the last walk. Then all of a sudden my Mama hugged me. I thought this was her saying good-bye, but she whispered in my ear, "He pleaded guilty; you don't have to be a witness." My heart reentered my body from where it had been hanging on a hook above us. My sweat dried up, my limbs reattached from the white butcher paper, and the people turned to congratulate me on being "such a brave young man!" I was now a hero having saved Michael, Pat and Beth from child slaughter. Hiding in the car was such a brilliant idea one man said. I think I mumbled "thank you." I checked to see if I had peed on myself. I hadn't. After all my kidneys and pecker had been frozen in white butcher paper.

Back at school I was suddenly famous. When I got to Mrs. Vice's class she stopped her lesson and asked me to tell the story of The Pontiac and the Knife Man. I probably stretched a few facts, but I never told them about promising God about being a missionary. I hope He's not still mad at me. I became a teacher instead. About the same thing as a missionary, surely He knows that.

By the way, Ida Mae's pig got too big for the house, and so they killed and ate it. Our having "steps up to our back porch" made more sense to me now. Mama knew I couldn't handle us eating a pet.

20

Frankincense smells like a Florida Queen cigar

Today is Christmas 1957. I am twelve, once again, I didn't get to play Mary in the church pageant. I get to play a lovely shepherd (my Indian print bathrobe plus some well-rope wrapped around one of Mama's best towels – color coordinated by me – on my short-haired head. I still have the bathrobe!). And of course, no sheep. No sheep doo-doo in the church, thank you. At that age I thought goats were sheep. Plenty of goats were around, but they were too wild, and anyway they would have eaten the Baby Jesus doll. My parents probably told me the difference, but I blocked that useful knowledge out. Sheep, goats – there was no "dividing the left from the right" for me. I was "saved."

One time I almost got Ruffles, our Cocker Spaniel, to be approved as a sheep substitute, but that lasted all of one rehearsal, during which he kept sniffing the Baby Jesus doll in the manger. No dogs as sheep. Too vulgar. Too much like goats. When I was older, I played Gaspar, one of the wise men, and wore some relative's silk smoking jacket, my Aunt Lupearl's fur collar, a crown made of tin foil and cardboard (I still have the crown.). My "frankincense" was in a Florida Queen cigar box with rice glued all over it and spray painted silver. When I opened it for the Baby Jesus, "Joseph" smiled at me when he saw the Florida Queen's picture on the inside lid. I had forgotten to paint over her. "Joseph" was a cigar smoker. I handed him the

Christmas 1957

box. I remember him taking the box, opening it, and smelling the inside. Baby Jesus didn't stand a chance on getting that frankincense. Joseph was played by our preacher. No one knew he smoked. I did.

But I secretly wanted to play Mary. She was the star. All that "Round-yon-virgin" celebrity stuff. And for as long as I played various denizens of Bethlehem, I was hoping each year to be asked to play Mary. I never realized why I couldn't. Putnam was so small, the thought of cross-dressing would echo of outside world weirdness, and so I was ignored for my own sake. I was odd enough. Ronald as Mary never made it into the Christmas church program. Thank God my parents protected me all they could. The green Dotted Swiss recital dress was enough sartorial splendor for a young white boy to be forgiven for. After all, Mary was the mother of God. I didn't deserve the honor. I was lucky just to be in her presence.

The church building was kind of an annex to our house. A big room built on to our house although it was about a half a mile away. Sorta like kitchens built away from the main house in case the wood burning stove burned the biscuits along with the rest of the house. Even though we drove there, the church building seemed to still be on our property. Daddy being head deacon automatically made Mama the keeper of the Communion stuff. Little glass goblets for the grape drink and silver plated trays for the crackers. Jesus's blood was at least ten Grapico bottles all poured into this wonderful cut glass decanter with the faceted stopper. My sister still has it. The Holy Grail sits in her foyer.

The infinitesimal amount of Grapico and that tiny corner of a cracker never was clear to me. I was always hungry. I thought the "last supper" meant supper. My hand was slapped many times for trying to eat ALL of Jesus when the plate came to me. I figured out way late in life the reason I sat next to my mother during Communion. "Don't be greedy" always meant punishment to me. Still does.

Yet when we were going home after church, and I was in the back of the car, with the left over saltine body parts, I was never stopped from drinking the rest of His blood or eating His remaining flesh. Thank goodness Mama used saltines from the house. Other churches, I found out, used crackers without salt.

I take blood pressure medicine now, probably because my love of salt started in the church, when it stood for much more than sustenance. Saltines were manna from Heaven, the body of Jesus, the private feast in the back seat, and the fact that I got to eat more than just a corner of His salvation.

Being the head deacon's son was a mixed blessing, but I still count them. They're numberless.

99

21

She dropped out of heaven

She arrived at our house that summer on her way from Heaven to Earth and went straight into my heart. She wore a sleeveless, navy blue shirt-waist dress, with big white buttons all the way down the front. That's how vivid my memory of her is. Her arms grew out of the dress like featherless wings, and reached towards me in a double hand held greeting. Her touch, along with her smell of Jungle Gardenia perfume, took hold of my boy brain, and I felt, looking up into her angel face, a rush that I've rarely felt since. Maybe when I was… no, never since.

She was the Vacation Bible School worker sent from the Baptist Bethel Association to lead the VBS that week in early

June. I was eleven, and love was something I had for my folks, maybe sometimes for my sisters, for Margaret and for Junior in particular. She was a different love – confusing and dangerous. She was to stay with us (because of my sisters), and I had to sleep upstairs where the Boogerman lived. She made the Boogerman disappear from my life that summer. Knowing she was downstairs negated him stealing my soul and spitting out my bones after he had eaten me slowly, so I would feel each bite. For her to wipe that fear from me made her God. Well, at least an angel – in a shirt-waist dress.

Vacation Bible School was so heady because it was the first week after school was out. I was free to play with Junior for three months. Summer vacations were from my birthday, May 23rd (It was the best birthday present I got, and I got it every year!), to after Labor Day. Real time for children to play. Real time for growing up in lazy wildness. So VBS was like the starting gate. I knew what was ahead. Lots of summer. Lots of it. Up to her arrival, I had treated VBS with religious indifference and pre-summer patience. We had Big Mama's free store-bought oatmeal cookies (they owned a general store). Kool-Aid,

and banana popsicles for recess. We made popsicle stick bowls, all stacked in a hexagon, bird houses out of pre-cut pieces of Daddy's wood, plywood book ends (my favorite, that I still have, were apple shapes we got to jig-saw out. I think they're apples…it was a hand held jig-saw), cutting boards (shellacked plywood - still have one), and various Jesus knick-knacks to keep us aware of why we were having so much fun. We prayed a lot, mostly for thanks.

But she changed it all. I worked on all the projects to please her. I memorized so many Bible verses, that when we had a Sword Drill (to defend ourselves with God's word against the Devil), I won every time, and the other kids thought I was a Bible verse smart ass and hated me. I would blurt out the memorized verse so fast and loud when she called out the chapter and verse that I had to be calmed down. To please her was to please the Heavenly Father. During the commencement program, at the end of the week, no other child wanted to perform the final Sword Drill because I had memorized almost the entire New Testament. I alone would be featured as a monologist, reciting entire chapters! Acting crept into the wooing of her love, after all, my script was some of the best writing ever written! There was no judging. There was no forgetting lines. Matthew, Mark, Luke, etc were my prompters. She was my muse. The church pulpit was my first stage. What a debut!

She made me a Royal Ambassador. Those are like Princes with Christ being the King. I hallucinated. Crowns hovered over our heads. Purple velevet robes trimmed in white ermine dotted with their little black tail tips floated around our shoulders, never touching, as if for show. I knew about ermine from fifth grade life science. They were brown ratty weasels that turned white in winter with those little black tips nestled in the white fur of royalty. Somewhere in the Yukon, on a tundra in Canada, or around my shoulders they finally lay, adorning me in splendor for Christ, and mostly for her. I was so in love, my flights of fancy were tinged with true madness. I think my parents worried so much about my sanity during that summer, that perhaps I should (as they often said) "be seen about." But the week flew by and the madness soon faded into June deliciousness. She never left completely. She's still way back there in the euphoria part of my brain. Today she would be called a dopamine rush. I simply called it love. After all, my favorite verse during a Sword Drill was "God is Love."

She was His word made flesh.

Putnam Baptist Church

22

The Carolina Biological Supply Co. tour

I love skulls. Bleached, symmetrical, brain-lost, bone coffins hung on walls, resting on steps, adorning witch doctor headdresses, or simply discovered at the edge of a pond or under a Yaupon bush in an old field. I collected them growing up in Putnam. Lots of fields, lots of web-of-life deaths and lots of time on hand to run around sixty five acres of property rich in pastures and woods. Dog skulls with bullet holes right smack dab in the middle between the eyes, where Daddy had sent a dying or cripple pet to its own heaven. Those were my favorite. The off-center ones bothered me. As if the dog might have suffered more, or happened to look at Daddy too late.

If I found the carcass before the maggots and crows and buzzards had cleaned it to that saffron color before sun bleaching, and its hair was still glued on to its bones like an unfinished pagan art project, Daddy would show me how to bury it in a fire ant bed and wait for a few weeks. The wait was agonizing. Every chance I'd get, I'd sneak away from the house to look. I learned to wait. Ants don't ask for the stinking piece of dog to be put in their bed. They cleaned it when everything else was done. Like raising 600 billion more fire ants. At least that's what I imagined. I was a child out of the last Ice Age. Bones were as valuable to me as toy trucks were to other little boys. Nobody in their right mind would want to watch the art of decay like me. But I learned early in my obsession not to brag about how many dog skulls I had. I still wanted a couple of kids to come to my birthday parties.

My favorite discovery of bones was one summer when the pond lost about a third of its water from a dry spell, and there at the edge of the new level was the complete skeleton of a beaver. I watched it for several weeks as the sun bleached what had been stripped by pond critters. The vertebrae were all clean, but arranged like jagged pearls in a semicircle around the snout of its head. It looked like a burial ritual with that arrangement at the head and the other bones, femurs, radials, ulnae, tarsals, scattered like they had been thrown there by the Pond God divining the future of the beaver's family. Well that's what it looked like to me. Fearing a rain or a neighbor bone collector, I picked up all that were bleached and saved them for years. A major reason I majored in biology were the bones. The beautiful, creepy, tiny wired together animal specimens under bell jars in my college labs told me secretly - I imagined they would turn toward me when I was alone with them and nod - that I had chosen the right profession. Bone Teacher. Bone labeler. Mr.

Harris, Skull Fancier.

I would spend hours perusing the Carolina Biological Supply Company catalog, finding every conceivable reason to order the rhesus monkey skeleton or the golden lion tamarind macaque. They cost hundreds of dollars, and I knew I could teach worlds about them to my students. The head of the biology department never bought them or my "lesson plans." We did good to get a small skeleton of a frog. The closest thing to exotica in a bell jar was a Norway rat. I had no desire to teach of its habitat. No one cared about Norway anyway. At least I didn't. I was interested in jungles and macaws and indigenous people with feathered headdresses who ate monkey brains. Norway? Rats? Forget it.

But the planets lined up for me one weekend in graduate school at the University of Georgia. A field trip to study plants in the Smokies came along with a side trip tour of the Carolina Biological Supply Company! It was better than a trip to the moon. I was going to be in room after room of rhesus, macaques, howlers, gibbons, chimps. Maybe there would be free samples. I had my list.

The tour guide assumed we were all anatomy students, not botanists, so we began what is still my favorite adventure in scientific weirdness.

Room One:
Freezers. A room full of freezers: uprights, lift tops, walk-ins. Cold as Norway! Sterile as a holding room for astronauts returning from Mars. Did I mention cold? Why were we in a showroom for Frigidaires?

The guide walked to the first lift-top. Our party of six followed. He opened the lid. We came closer. There on top, with its arms open toward us and covered in frost, was a male blue face mandrill baboon, mouth open in its last primal scream, reaching to pull us down into its frozen hell. We gasped at intervals as we realized the freezer was full of them. All in various positions like a stuffed monkey display at FAO Schwartz … in Norway.

The guide explained the carnage; crates of exotic animals seized by customs officials at international airports. Or pets gone wild or too dangerous to keep. This was the fall of 1970. In the late 50s and early 60s you could still order most of what we saw that day from the Spiegel catalog. I know. I have one from 1959. What we saw that day! What a simple statement. Like a diary entry from a day on vacation.

We continued on our tour. Mr. Guide asked us what kind of animals we were interested in. Oh, I don't know. A wooly mammoth? A saber tooth tiger perhaps? After this first treat, I was a kid in a bone store. With 50 cents burning in my pocket.

The uprights housed a leopard. One held a chimpanzee. I was so excited and freaked out at the same time that I don't remember what all he showed us. I still couldn't get the mandrill's blue frosted face and its yellow fangs out of my head.

He told us the walk-ins had horses, pigs, and cows for veterinary schools. No interest to me. Those were on our farm in Putnam. Some of the group stepped in there, but I didn't. I asked to see the baboon again. He let me. It seemed to have shifted. Delirium.

Room Two:
Butchers. Several men in white lab coats carving the meat off the thawed out carcasses. Long stainless steel tables, lots of clinking sounds of knives, saws, scalpels being placed on the metal tables. No talking. These were bone merchants, peeling away skin, offal, muscle to get to the treasure: bones. We didn't stay in there long, didn't need to. This was close to watching

someone dissect your favorite pet or Bagheera or Thumper. None of the butchers looked up. At the end of the day they probably all cried in their beers and told dead pet stories. My imagination was in overdrive.

Room Three:
It was like an oven. A conveyer belt (there would be many more to come) ran through the far side of the room. On the belt were stripped animals. Just tendons or ligament fragments hanging on partially scrapped bones. The belt was an open grid of stainless steel mesh and underneath it a long pan collecting the grease dripping from the now collapsed carcasses. It was so hot we got only a glimpse of the process. Seeing those butchered exotic animals moving horizontally across the end of the room was like a macabre shooting game at a carnival. None of us wanted to stay there any longer. The smell alone had us looking for the exit.

Room Four:
"Oh, the horror, the horror!"
I mentioned the bad smell in Room Three. The guide told us if that room offended anyone, we shouldn't even consider going into the next one. Well, he had not taken Reverse Psychology 101. We all stood in front of Room Four grinning like Cheshire cats, all smiles and no bodies. Irony overload.

We were excited. It was a smaller room, so we went in by twos. Mr. Guide tried to describe the room clinically. We would see barrels, lots of them,scattered around the room, and the temperature would be about 120 degrees. We were to choose one or two barrels to look in and then come back out because, we were warned, people had passed out in there from the heat. Some chose not to go in, but I had to. I was about to enter a

tropical jungle of the dead. I was chomping at the bit. The guide
had mentioned something about beetles. Dermestid beetles. In
barrels. Nature's cannibals. Flesh eaters. But small, non-flying.
OK – so far.

What he failed to mention was how the Dermestid beetles
were in the thousands. In each barrel. And what he failed to
mention was the noise. Their bodies slamming into each other.
Their lack of table manners. Oh, yes, he also never to mentioned
the stench.

I went in.

Imagine first … my Baptist vision of Hell. Unbearably hot,
cacophonous and frenetic.

Now take away the frenetic. This hell was contained in
barrels. Oil drum size, beer keg size, pickle bucket size. Go to
only two, look in, and come back out, we were instructed.

The stench, plus the heat, seared our lungs. We could taste
the rot. We could hear a drone like a hive of bees on steroids.
It was so disorienting that I had second thoughts. No, by God,
I was going to look into one of the mouths of Hell. Go for the
biggest barrel. By now I was holding my breath. I looked in.

There, because of its size, propped up against the side of
the barrel, was the yellowed skull of a chimpanzee, or some
larger primate, and that was all I saw of it. The rest of its body
was covered by black enameled, dome shaped, headless beetles,
moving like speeded up film on amphetamine-laced crack.
Millions of them. I don't know whether it was the lack of oxygen
in my lungs or the shock of the cruelty of nature, but I almost
passed out. What snapped me back to the "fight or flight" vagus
nerve-safety-back-up was the sound over the din of the skeleton
collapsing into the bottom of the barrel. I had smoked the mescal
of the shaman and seen the end of time. I was out of there with
no memory of fleeing. The color and saucer-eyed expression

on our faces said enough. It took us several minutes to find our bearings. I kept feeling things in my clothes. I was afraid to look, so with eyes straight ahead, we went to the next room.

Room Five:

Quiet. Peaceful. Empty.

Except for another conveyor belt, this one behind a glass enclosed section, again moving toward some endless destiny, this one not in Norway. I had grown used to infinity being redefined. The silence was shocking. Because of the glass partition, even the drone of the mechanical part of this death tour was missing. Then I saw another conveyor belt beneath the top one moving in the opposite direction, going back into the beetle room. Empty.

Room Five was pure theatre. A set up. There were no specimens on either belt. We gathered and stared at the enclosed room. Then the drama began. A pile of bones entered from the left, covered in Dermestid beetles. They had devoured all connecting tissues but were still clinging on, hoping for a bit of dessert hidden away in an eye socket or brain cavity. The bones were not covered totally as they were in the Hell Room, so the others in our group began to doubt our previous experience as hyperbole. Suddenly the beetles began to drop off the bones one by one and fall onto the belt going the opposite way beneath them. We looked at the tour guide. "Ether," he said.

The enclosed room was filled with ether. They were putting the little suckers to sleep and sending them back to the Hell Room. To feast again after waking up from their midday siesta after having stuffed themselves on monkey meat just minutes earlier. They'd found their food stamps forever!

It became the most surreal thing I had ever seen; watching a silent movie of black spots first scurrying all over a pile of bones then gradually all falling away until, at the end of the runway, the bones were beetle-less and scattered as though they were at the Oracle at Delphi.

Room Six:
We didn't go in there.
It was the bleaching room. No need to watch bones bleach. It would be too anticlimactic. I couldn't even begin to imagine the smell in there.

Room Seven:
The school of natural architecture.
The rebuilding of the Norway Rat, the Coatimundi, the Mandrill Baboon, the Clydesdale.
Men and women at stations with magnifying lamps, beautiful, strange, stainless steel tools, and wire and glue and skills as precise as diamond cutters. Quietly hunched over the eons of calcium, built up into the practical framework that holds the animal kingdom together. Bone carpenters creating visual sculptures for study and, in my case, for beauty, for joy.

Room Eight:
The display room where the bell jars and the glass boxes encased the finished products. We were seeing nature and craft perfectly combined. I felt such a mixture of joy and wonder that I experienced a new feeling for the first time. That innocence of discovery when I was a boy (the beaver by our dried out pond) plus the knowledge and privilege of what I had just witnessed, revealed to me an epiphany of nature as both real and spiritual. Of bones as life and beauty, as something we can hold and sense more than just its formation and purpose, but also as their connection to us. Seeing skeletons there in their perfection, I couldn't help but feel a closeness to whatever – or

Whomever – placed us all here together.

Room Nine:

This was the end of our tour, where all the larger animals for the veterinary schools were stored. Shelf after shelf of pigs, horses, cows, sheep, dogs and cats. By this time I was so overwhelmed that I had forgotten to ask about free samples. On the way out, the guide said if anyone was interested, there was a box of damaged skulls and turtle shells at the exit. My heart flipped. I was the only one who stopped at the box. The others were botanists, remember.

I left with my first otter and my second beaver skull. The beaver skull looked much smaller than my first one, from when I was a boy. But then again, when you're small, everything is larger than life.

Mr. Boy 1974

23

Skullduggery: The death of Smokey

Smokey was my Daddy's garden mule, but he was actually a Shetland pony. My Shetland pony. The one I rode into Jerusalem on Palm Sunday that spring, or simply translated into "riding through Putnam with Daddy's cows following on our way up to Big Daddy's pasture."

He died from choking on a corncob one Sunday. Even when the county veterinarian came all the way from Linden, 30 miles away, and he and Daddy, using our garden hose, tried to dislodge it from his throat, he died. Sitting on the fence and watching two grown men using simply what was at hand, try desperately to save him, I was overwhelmed with helplessness. As they stood up and pulled the hose from Smokey's throat, I saw in my father

Daddy & Smokey

and his friend, Mr. Billy Austin, my first realization that my strong-willed Daddy was not afraid to grieve. I had been to many funerals with him, and he had never flinched from his stoical countenance. But today he was visibly saddened. So was Mr. Austin. They dragged Smokey to the back of the barn, and as the vet walked toward his car, I sensed he felt he had lost a patient.

So, after many months of weather, and nature's scavengers doing their efficient work, Smokey turned from my pet into his other form, the white scaffolding of remembrance.

I took his head, now separated from the rest of his bones – probably by two buzzards arguing over dinner or a stray dog trying to survive – and buried it in the biggest fire ant hill in the pasture. The routine. Waiting. And waiting. His head was massive, even for a Shetland pony, and I was used to dog or cat sized skulls. I never kept the lower jaw of my skulls, too life-like.

But I kept Smokey's.

A Clorox solution in a number two washtub, a soaking of days, and using the same hose the vet used trying to save him, I prepped him for posterity. That was sometime in the 1970s. His skull is resting now in the middle of a tableau on my back deck.

I have a trip to Greece planned for this summer. I'm taking two or three of Smokey's teeth with me. I'll find a spot off from the crowd at Delphi and cast them there on hallowed ground. I'll "read" them and find out my future.

When I get back home I'll replace them into Smokey's skull. It will lie there the same as before.

And one cold day, when the green algea that coats his skull in summer is killed off by winter's bleach, I'll tell him what the Oracle whispered to me.

24

Haints, priscillas curtains & wisdom

My Daddy's Mama, Big Mama, ended my childhood foolishness. Their house had been struck by lightning and burned to the ground. It was the palace of my fondest pleasures. Mayonnaise and saltine cracker sandwiches as reward for being good. Sitting alone at her table in the kitchen, built away from the house, cold in winter, insufferably hot in summer, didn't matter. I sat there alone, eating the oil and salt of good behavior. I always was on good behavior with Big Mama. She was without fault, smelled good, and loved me the most. So my grandfather Big Daddy said as she lay dying from a stroke. "You were her favorite," he grumbled. He never liked me. Maybe it was the green Dotted

Big Mama

Swiss recital dress.

Anyway, after the fire, they lived with us while their new little brick house was being built. They had forever lived in the big white enclosed dog-trot clapboard built millions of years before, and when they moved into the compact brick bungalow with too-low ceilings, they seemed to get much smaller and less grand. It was so sad to me to see my perfect grandmother become ordinary and small. I missed the crackers in so many ways. The only thing I remember from the ashes that day was how the white metal cabinet that held her dishes had burned black with all her white cheap china melted into a strange shaped heap, sticking up from the black ruins like solid white water trying to puddle there in the ashes.

While they were at our house for about six months, my favorite holiday arrived - Halloween. I was home from college, then called Alabama College, now the University of Montevallo, and met up with Junior for what turned out to be our last shameless dive into madness. Upstairs, my Mama had tons of priscillas curtains adorning all the windows. Yards and yards of rayon frilliness that served no purpose but to be frilly and pretty for my Mama's pleasure. They also made great possibilities for dressing up "haints." Now, haints are southern ghosts that float out of graveyards and show up in dark corners or in a drunk's vision.

One time Ruffles, our cocker spaniel, somehow followed me to Junior's, and was hiding under Granny's stove when she walked in the kitchen. She saw his half hidden body, knew it was a haint, and screamed bloody murder. Pushed us all out of the house – Doog, Lemar, Coy, Junior, Jenny, and me – into a pouring down gully-washer rain. We stood forever until Ruffles appeared on the porch, grinning his silly dog grin, wagging his silly short stumped tail, and we all looked up at Granny as she turned to me and said, "Don't bring that dog to my house again. Bad luck for a dog in the house. Haints get into dogs and bring hoo-doo to your life." I always looked at Ruffles differently after that day.

The curtains begged for me to take them down, tie them around Junior and me, and go down to the cemetery, hide behind tombstones, and fly out across the graveyard when a car passed on its way to the Ginfield. The Ginfield was where most of the colored folks lived. Gin for cotton, gin for moonshine – it was never clear why they named it the Ginfield. But it was conveniently located past the cemetery. Now I'm scared shitless of the cemetery at night, but somehow, having been off at college, having had my first alcoholic drink, having God know what other firsts, I was emblazoned with new stupidity. Junior was game and glad to see me, and as always, never questioned my ideas. We had forgotten the electrocution, the scalded foot, the many whippings. We were into scaring the bejesus out of others.

As the cars approached, we commenced our frantic haint-waving antics, rising and running and hiding and laughing, collapsing on the ground, hallow until now, as people gunned their cars to the floorboard and raced wide eyed towards their safety.

When we drove back to the house (I had hidden our car in

some sweet gum trees behind the cemetery), we were ecstatic. Only Big Mama was home, and she asked us where we'd been. Proud of my cleverness, I told her.

Big Mama, maker of prized mayonnaise and cracker sandwiches, cross-word puzzle solver extraordinaire, and genuinely my favorite person on earth, spoke in a voice I had never heard. As her glare penetrated into my silly soul she said, "You boys are lucky to be alive. Haints can be killed you know. All you have to do is shoot them through the heart." One tries to pinpoint in life when life changes for good. That Halloween night, standing with Junior, holding those Priscillas curtains and facing my grandmother's metaphoric wisdom, I learned in my life the greatest lesson so far. Others' feelings and others' beliefs are to be revered and respected, and even if you get pleasure out of the moment, other people can kill you for your shenanigans – just by pointing a gun and shooting you through your silly heart.

25

The chicken and the Coach

I had a tenth-grade biology teacher named Miss Helen Young Lewis. She, of course, also taught P.E. Why biology and physical education were paired in my pedagogy was perhaps coincidental, or simply a warning. I hated P.E. classes, but I loved biology. As long as we got to dance in the gym on rainy days, I tolerated the physical of softball and the other "balls." Ronald vs. Contact Sports was always a painful exhibition game, both mentally and physically. I don't even remember being chosen for any sport team. I appreciated sitting all of them out. I wanted to be a cheerleader. One year, I even went for tryouts, much to the embarrassment of my sisters, both of whom were top-notch cheerleaders. Everyone tolerated Celia and Lena

Carol's younger brother; he was "cute." He also dreamed of those gored cheerleader skirts. But I digress.

Helen Young Lewis was the smartest person on the planet. She knew the scientific names of all the trees I had grown up under. *Pinus strobus, Pinus taeda, Pinus palustris* – my first romantic language. It still feels good to wax scientifically as I botanized in early spring. She also, knew how to dance. Smart, profound, shake-your-ass – the three reasons I became a biology teacher.

I should have known, arriving that first day of practice teaching at Ramsey High School in Birmingham during my last six weeks of college, that Biology always went with P.E. My supervising teacher during that practice teaching era was a coach. He greeted me the first morning, shook my hand – broke it – gave me the class rolls, the textbook, and then left. That was my training. I never saw him in the classroom again until the day we dissected chickens. Yes, chickens. Frogs, I knew; chickens were his specialty.

My college supervisor came the day of the chicken slaughter to observe my work. The coach had brought the victims from home: two Leghorn (*Gallus domesticus*) hens, in a cage, on his desk in the lab, ready for what I though would be models as he "dissected" a store-bought, skinned chicken. Not to be. As my college professor sat in the back, I assisted up front in my new, wash-and-wear 50% dacron, three-button, narrow notched lapel J.C. Penney suit. "Coach" proceeded to murder one of the pure white chicken victims in front of the class.

He took the first one out, rung its neck (yes, there in a public place of enlightenment) with blood spurting everywhere, plucked its feathers in a flurry of skill and vengeance, singed its remaining feather stubs over a Bunsen burner (imagine the smell, the carnage, the permanent adolescent mental damage on that day in May 1967) and then, with a butcher knife, sliced and pared, with the skill of a Germanic warlord from 932 A.D., the pink yielding flesh of a leghorn maiden.

I am certain that somewhere in Alabama there is a secret cult of thirty 57-to-58 year-olds who meet each May on an abandoned chicken farm, and sacrifice an innocent leghorn to the God of Chicken Torture. They all wear 60s wash-and-wear suits, smear the victim's blood across their foreheads and down their cheeks, chant the words, "leg, thigh, breast and bone, connect again and fly away home," in a futile effort to purge the curse inflicted on them by the guardians of higher learning. They burn an effigy of Colonel Sanders as their last purification rite and promise to always promote with vigor the advantages of home schooling and the damnation of Biology, P.E. and Public Education. They are all charter members of the Birmingham chapter of PETA.

When my college supervising professor left that day, with an ashed pallor and a weak voice, he shook my hand with both of his hands, held them in a prolonged moment of almost religious blessing, and said, "You'll get an A+, but you deserve much, much more." As he stared at the dot-matrix of chicken blood on my new suit, his grip got tighter. He finally released me when i said, "it's wash-and-wear."

I taught Biology, with profound love and excitement for twenty years after that. And, believe it or not, my favorite food is fried chicken. Popeye's: two drumsticks, biscuit, Cajun rice and sweet tea. I'm in the car now.

Lucky to be there

I danced with Shirley Jones, Betty White laid hands on my pulled groin muscle, Gordon McRae spit on my upturned face, and Robert Goulet smelled of aged Aqua Velva warmed by a fire in a honeymoon cabin built somewhere in the upper chambers of my naïve heart. It was summer stock just after I graduated from college in 1967, and I fell in love with the thought of theatre as a possible profession. I had my degree to be a Biology teacher, and theatre had been just playing around. That first summer, after the womb of college, jangled the molecules that, up to that point, had been just oxygen. What I breathed that summer was an isotope of rarefied air. I still have a whiff of its memory, but it never has been repeated.

It all started out as a Ronald-being-a-smartass and thinking he could dance. A bunch of us graduates, and a couple of theatre /music faculty took off for summer stock auditions for "Theatre Under the Stars," Atlanta's big name headliner summer theatre series. Chastain Park's reputation for being a regional showcase for celebrity vehicles was the place to be; only the best got to be one of twelve dancers (six guys, six girls) or twelve singers (same combination) to back up the stars. All literally and figuratively were doing theatre under the stars.

I just tagged along, not a singer, not a dancer, except for choir or a "mover" in our college dance club Orchesis. I sat there in the audience watching freakishly talented guys and girls sing like it was tryouts for the Heavenly Choir. Criminally beautiful, all of them. I became ashamed of the "melody" label my college choir director had branded me with. They were all angels, and it was so ridiculous me being there that my mind nearly snapped. The dance auditions were after lunch. I was joked on so much that this false sense of bravado swelled inside me to fight the whipping boy label. I had done some "character" dancing in Orchesis, had even been Lawrence in Maurice Jarre's theme from *Lawrence of Arabia* and thought I looked pretty damn swell in that white bed sheet. Hell, if Lawrence could "dance" and get people to follow him into the desert, why not Ronald in that old theatre somewhere on Peachtree Street?

I secretly borrowed one of the girl dancer's extra footless pair of tights and slipped out, found a bathroom and put them on under my pants and went back to the group sitting there cheering on the couple of girls who had come there to dance. As they called out for dancers to come to the stage (like in *A Chorus Line* all were taught the routine together) I stood, moved to the aisle and started taking off my pants. Several hearts stopped beating; mine was already somewhere with the Howeetats in the Sinai. My friends saw my tights and knew they had created Frankenstein's monster in spandex with their merciless taunting. It was much too late. The lever had been pulled. Lightning had channeled down the chandelier of that auditorium, ignited the spark of raw stupidity and hubris and given me the power to... dance!

To me it was just the prom in our high school gym, and I knew how to do the Twist. I had taken Social Dance as a P.E. elective in college and was pretty good at the Foxtrot. A crude Tango or a passable Two-Step was not enough to prepare me for a barrage of tour jetes , pas de bourrées and rond de jambes. All the instructions were French ballet terms that even the Rossetta stone couldn't have deciphered for me. I needed a translator who sold Quaaludes. I was as lost as Cooter Buck; a term Mama used when we were in Meridian, Mississippi, or Selma, Alabama, trying to find a new doctor's address. Daddy would say we were not lost just bewildered... I was both.

So I did what any coward would do... I moved to the back row, upstage in the darkening space of weaker shadows. As the lines moved forward to be skewered, I kept moving back furiously trying to learn from the feet and angles in front of me what all that French shit meant. I soon ran out of backing up. Our row was last and least.

Nothing to lose but my pride, my ride home, my future chance to get any Christmas or Birthday presents from my now ex-friends, and most of all, my sexuality. I was suddenly without genitalia, flailing around in a girl's footless black tights among a row of girly boys in dance belts and tiny, tight, white tee shirts that I am sure were their sisters. I was neutered, emasculated, and in a firing line with all the usual suspects who were sexless and perfectly coiffed. So I did the only thing left to do when you are about two inches high and shrinking. I broke loose with the appropriate steps, but my body was a Howdy Doody marionette manipulated by a drunk with Parkinson's.

The stoic, dead-faced sissy boys dancing to my left, lost their concentrated spot focus, and at the end of the routine, they moved away from me like I wore a sign that said, "Dancing Leper. Please Put Out of his Misery."

When the worst thing that can happen happens, you are quite numb. Walking back to the group in the back seemed to be about 300 miles in the dark and to a motel that says "No Vacancy." My precious friends all stared forward. Some had left during the train wreck and had conveniently gone to "get coffee." I sat away from the ones left and wondered if I had enough money for a Trailways bus ticket home. As I gave the tights back to my co-conspirator, she forced a smile. It was the only one I got the rest of the day.

And then the impossible happened. What a cliché. But there's no other word than impossible. The twelve singers were called forth. They stood magnanimous in a row of hugs and pats and handshakes and "I-will-be-your-lover-before-the-second-week-of-rehearsal" looks. I was in love with all of them. One named Marc Beavers was the most beautiful angel I had ever seen. There had been many pictured in my illustrated Bible at my home in Putnam. I thought he was Apollo. His father, I'm sure, was Zeus. I fantasized about him going down the line and choosing his bride that very day. Sons of gods can do that you know. One of the other guys was a voice professor at the University of Montevallo. He had ridden with us and sat with us before I danced. I hadn't seen him all the rest of the afternoon. I wondered if he had the power to revoke my degree due to the embarrassment I had inflicted on the university. Seeing him in line reduced my size to just ¾ of an inch. Another ½ inch and I would be ¼ of an inch from floor wax.

The dancers were called. I had become a vapor, an exhale, a cipher. I came to when my friend the co-conspirator, was shaking me. Her lips said something like, "Ronald, Ronald... they're calling your name! Oh my God, they're calling you to the stage!" In slo-mo I turned to the stage. The choreographer was at the mike, "Is Ronald Harris in the house?" I sucked in what little oxygen that had been left in the auditorium. My group and the stunned others left in their seats had already depleted 99% of the air. What I had left gave me a chance to see the other eleven dancer boys and girls simultaneously try to breathe in a reality that also hit me so hard the only explanation was that the cosmos had hicupped and memory had been blipped from all humanity at the same nanosecond.

As I glided to the stage, the realization of two things set in: number one; I was going to be totally lost in that dancer world, and number two; I was going to be in the presence of all those beautiful people for two and a half months. This realization poured into me like Boone's Farm Strawberry Hill wine, sweet, fruity and as quick a drunk as is earthly possible. I stood there beaming, an idiot grin that stretched across that stage and landed smack on Marc Beaver's face. When I turned to the other twenty three angels, he grinned back. I knew if Apollo approved, I was a demi-god.

The ride home was curiously silent, like a recount or a total re-election was needed. My winning a slot was not even discussed. I kept wondering if we were just now going over to Atlanta, not coming back home. I felt like saying, "I had this dream..."

The summer schedule of 1967. It started off badly. I had misread the first date of rehearsal to be the first day of June, which was right. Well there was orientation on the day before. I missed it. Already behind, a non-dancer, and Ronald couldn't read. I had done my practice teaching from the day after I got back from Atlanta in March up to graduation in May, six weeks of the most paradigm shifting imaginable. Graduation, getting a job for the Fall, bragging to every stranger I met about dancing with stars and angels, and prepping my parents for living in "Hotlanta" with "theatre people" burned a massive logic hole in my brain. So I missed the first day of summer stock paying no attention to May 31st as orientation and housing and assignments and general know-to-survive in a frenzied world of rehearsing one show during the day and performing a different show at night. Room assignment had already been chosen, and one sweet, kind boy held out for the Alabama idiot that might show up. He was my savior. Late into the night he would patiently go over routines with me to catch me up. Little did he know that I would need him every night. I think God sent him from his Special Needs Saints army.

At the end of the first week when I had killed myself to catch up and slept very little, I finally looked the choreographer in the eye for the first time and pitifully asked, "Why did you chose me? I know I'm a big disappointment." He, with his proverbal neck towel and turned-out stance, took me by the shoulders and stared into the back of my brain and said, "Because you didn't look like the other dancers. You can move. I needed a character dancer. I needed a fool. I mean that in the best way." The sun threw out a prominence bigger than recorded time and all communication equipment on Earth crackled for a moment. People all over the planet looked up from their coffee and their careers and perceived a slight change in the rooms where their lives had settled, a change for the better, an okay, a yes. He made me feel the same as Marc Beaver's grin had. And Marc being in the room was enough to rest my profound doubt and kick me up to first class to fly where the drinks were free.

The assimilation became easier as my confidence rose, and soon I was given little show bits that showcased my goofiness. I worked hard at being professionally retarded. We always rehearsed with a stand-in who came two weeks before the star arrived because we had only three days to work with the celebrity. The stars did the same blocking and choreography across the country. Shirley Jones was the first. I had loved her from the *Oklahoma!* and *Carousel* movies. The Oscar turn in *Elmer Gantry,* her voice, her beauty, her wonderful reputation. And I was chosen to be the one to hold her in the dance where all six of us guys lined up behind each other and danced as her partners. I held on to the stand-in for a week asking where to touch, how hard to dip, and where to look. I was scared *merde*less!

The day came. She walked in the room shaking everyone's hand down this long line of star-struck novices. A blue, some kind of heavenly blue scarf was tied around her neck. She had on rehearsal clothes, worn-in dance shoes, and no make-up. We couldn't breathe. A "thing" happened that day. I call it a thing because no previous or rarely since thing had happened to me. Once while on Sappelo Island off the coast of Georgia, I saw three deer on a sand dune silhouetted against a low, full moon. Once on the beach alone at Gulf Islands National Seashore, as I lay half in the surf, a great blue heron walked up next to my head and stood there looking for a fish he'd spotted swimming around my feet. He stood there looking for a minute or for eternity and then rushed with wings out towards its victim. And once as I walked through a narrow, rocked passage in remote Turkey, the bas-reliefed Hittite warriors marching to oblivion on either side of me seemed to turn their half heads to me and become released from their granite grave as they looked down at me. Time stopped. Those were the four "things" that have happened to me.

So I loved Shirley Jones. In fact before her weekly run of *On a Clear Day You Can See Forever,* I was slipping into her dressing room and with my own theater lipstick, was writing "I love you" on her mirror. She was that accessible. She was that perfect. One night it started to flood. This was "Theatre Under the Stars" so there was no cover over the stage or the audience. As the hundreds of umbrellas began to make a popping, black ceiling of circles over the patrons, the stage had puddles we dancers couldn't avoid. The number where we all danced with her ended abruptly when one dancer slipped and we all crashed into the stage like soaked dominoes. I let go so as not to pull Miss Jones down with us, and at this point the show must *not* go on. The producer's policy was to stick out the first act to intermission, then the tickets didn't have to be refunded. With a great laugh, dealing with the fact we were doing *On a Clear Day,* Miss Jones looked at us then up at the sky and called for her yellow rain slicker and an umbrella and told us, still in the wet heap, and the audience, that the show had to stop but she would take requests from the audience. She had a repertoire already prepared in case this happened, and there in her Morton salt outfit, she and the orchestra, with huge umbrellas covering them, went through the "If I Loved You" and "People Will Say We're in Love" and ending with "On a Clear Day." All of us forgot the rain and stood in the wings without umbrellas and watched that voice stop the gods from crying. We acolytes got to be near greatness, and the congregation got their prayers answered. The only one disappointed was the producer and his wallet. I'm sure the audience came back sometimes in the run to see the rest of the musical. When I hear "On a Clear Day" now on satellite radio's Broadway channel, this "thing" happens all over again. Not exactly like the first time, but just as powerful as those deer, that heron, and those Hittites turning to notice me as a fellow traveler trekking on in terra incognito lit by an overhead light of stardust.

And then there was Betty White "laying hands" on my pulled groin muscle. She and Allen Ludden were Sarah Brown and Sky Masterson in *Guys and Dolls*. Atlanta was their first venue on the tour so we got them for a full two weeks. Allen Ludden was the one I knew because of *Password*. I didn't know much about Betty White, but it only took five minutes in the room with her pretending she was dim-witted and so smart at the same time to convince all of us she was Lucille Ball, Gracie Allen and Imogene Coca cloned into one crazy, smart, funny, beautiful clown. No stand-ins, the real McCoys everyday, nine to five. As the 60s turned into the 70s, into the 80s, into the 90s, into the aughts, and especially her zenith in 2010, and possibly forever, there she still remains, top funny banana. "Lucky to have been there" is still my mantra.

Guys and Dolls has a wild Havana dance number that evolves into a drunken brawl. Of course it was choreographed to the Nines. I didn't warm up properly one night and during a leap from a table to a rehearsed "one million times" landing on another dancer's back, we collapsed wrong and I pulled my left side groin muscle. I felt this pop inside my crotch and knew it was something we had been drilled about. Warm up till you sweat or else. The else happened. I survived the dance but was sidelined for the rest of the show and unfortunately for several days during rehearsal for the next show, *Funny Girl*. On a previous night one dancer got a stilleto heel imbedded through his barefoot sandal and limped off stage with the shoe riding on the top of his foot like some sort of sick "what's wrong with the picture?" He was out for the run of the show. That and my groin injury caused the show to be re-choreographed; there were only four guy dancers and it was a partner kind of number. Miss White and Mr. Ludden became knock-about nurses to me and the other injured guy, bouncing off jabs and quips about groins and groans, missteps, stilettos, and "shoe-ins" until we hurt in a welcomed way. They were true members of an ensemble that made it the best show of the season.

Wanting to impress my fellow summer stock friends in other shows like *Horn in the West* or *The Stephen Foster Story* when they came for their brief breaks, I convinced my choreographer to let me dance the Havana number one more time in the last performance. He did and I wished he hadn't. My leg was still black from the blood that leaked under my skin, but I had shown it to no one. My lack of respect for my body stopped after that night. I defied the doctor and lost. The same moment in the dance, the same move, the same muscle ripped again. I collapsed on stage and they dragged me off – in character. At intermission the announcement came, "Is there a doctor in the house?"

I was in the dressing room, lying on a make-up table in such a state that my pain rivalled my stupidity. A doctor entered and asked me where it hurt. I had been stripped and everyone saw the black bruise inside my thigh and wondered if the doctor was blind. He said, swear to God "I'm a psychiatrist. You need a real doctor." No shit Dr. Freud! Miss White and Allen Ludden rushed in, came over to the black legged boy in the dance belt and nothing else. She grabbed my hand, looked at the eggplant the size of Texas under my skin and said, "How did you hurt your arm?" I blurted through tears and snot and shame, "It's my leg, Miss White!" without missing the Comedy 101 beat, she looked up at Allen Ludden and said, "I always get them mixed up!" For a split second the laughter in the room anesthetized my eggplant, and I was not the cadaver in Eakins's *The Gross Clinic* but the "ba dum bum" of her comic timing. A real doctor arrived and we went to the hospital. A hospital gown, a dance belt, a punch line. Betty White could then, and still now, produce the zinger of all zingers. To meet her again is on my bucket list. She's incomparable.

Next up was *Kismet* with Gordon MacRae. We'd had Laurie from *Oklahoma* and then, the second month up rode Curly. Trouble was Curly was a spitter. Songs projected out of his mouth like liquid rockets. His notes soared into the stratosphere with a comet's tail of crooner spittal. We underlings, all prostate at his feet as slaves to the Hajj the Poet, would shield our faces, like unworthy peons forced to entertain the mighty, when we were really protecting ourselves from Mr. MacRae's saliva rain. One night in his full bellicosity, I was distracted. What had distracted me was that I had committed a cardinal sin of the theatre. I had forgotten part of my costume, my turban. We would get fined $25 (a lot of money in 1967) for a missing part of a costume. I was in more deep doo-doo; I had no protection from Mr. Deluge. And of course I was nearest to his feet. And it came as expected, but it seemed he wanted me punished along with the garnishee of my wages. Or maybe I just really wanted to be drawn and quartered for my lack of professionalism. (Remember I was still trying to compensate to some of the cast members for being an inbred from the family tree of the Beverly Hillbillies.) Well, the size of the glob was between mothball and golf ball. It sailed past my upturned palm and caught me between the temple and the hairline. It had a sound. My left ear, just one inch away from the projectile, recorded an impact sound of Jell-O dropped from ten feet onto a tympani drum. As the splattered Jell-O bathed my entire left cheek in celebrity DNA, I wished very hard, and perhaps prayed, for the unspoken word: Rain! It didn't come. I wore Mr. MacRae's mark of Cain until the number was over. The words "spit shine" took on new meaning. I exited to my dressing room to change, wipe the spittle residue, and sure enough, the stage manager had posted the $25 fine on my mirror. Others who saw what had happened made sure I had my turban on for the rest of the run. But none of them loved me enough to sit next to his feet. After all I had been chosen to hold Laurie when the others had not. I deserved Curly who sang "Everything's going my way!"

Robert Goulet came with his own show. He was so big at the time that he didn't need back-up dancers or singers. His voice was all that the throngs came to hear, and his beauty was enough for them to see. It was not past glory, he *was* glory. There's not much to tell about his presence "under the stars" except all twenty four of us would come to the theatre night after night, stand in the wings and watch him command the night. He was polite to us and we knew to keep our distance. He would walk passed us so focused on his power to entertain that there was no eye contact. We were props, but not in a sarcastic way. We were just not needed. When he walked by he smelled so good that both the guys and the girls talked about his scent. It was never described just right. I couldn't tell you what it was comparable to. I suspect his completely beautiful being-voice, face, body, clothes, coolness, and passion-made us sense something none of us had ever been around. He was such a stunning package of what we 24 all had separately. He humbled the most egotistical and inspired the hardest workers to work harder. When he died in 2007 after several years of faded glory, I felt very lucky to have been in the theatre with him, to have experienced the entertainer, at his peak, to have been in the wings, to have had the honor of being among friends trying to describe the sweet smell of success. I know one thing; it smelled really, really good.

Coda: *Funny Girl*

Did I mention I couldn't really dance? Well the word dance is one thing, general, subjective, all encompassing. But then there's Tap. Try faking Tap. You see, the visual is accompanied by precise, objective syncopated Loud Noise.

We were all 12 lined up kick line across the stage for the "Rat-a-tat" number, decked out in genuine World War I wool uniforms, Dough boy hats, gaiters, boots, the whole nine yards. During rehearsals I didn't have tap shoes so they assumed I was in sync. That's how smoke and mirrors I had become. But when we put on those heavy real World War I army boots festooned in taps that looked like Inquisition silver half moons – massive, sandwiched metal with screw heads the size of dimes – my magic was over. The rabbit was dead.

I heard the tapping rhythm in my head, thinking that would be channeled into my feet. You can't think tap and it just works. I had seen *The Music Man* and tried to think "Rat-a-tat" into my feet. I'd forgotten that also it was fiction.

We had gotten only into about eight counts of the dance routine when the choreographer's bull horn, way out there in the back row of the park seating blasted, "Stop!" I felt my stomach flip flop. Imagine outside in July heat, in the South, in World War I full regalia, 12 people arm-to arm, sweating profusely. It happened as I expected. The choreographer called out, "Someone take the taps off Ronald Harris's boots!" I was used to the summer-long barrage of snickers but his command erupted into a complete laugh track. Eleven "Dough Boys" collapsed in heaps of army wool, temporarily forgetting their misery. By this time in the summer I had become a punch line. I was the only one standing as three stage hands approached; two to hold me up and one with a Philips head screwdriver. Imagine the tableau: me raising my feet backwards, one at a time, being held by grinning, sweaty, burly, bearded stage hands; facing the empty sea of seats except for the doubled over choreographer; eleven laughing dancers by now drinking water brought by other stage hands, and me being de-screwed in a tap dance ritual that began and ended that day in July 1967.

Wonder if the *Guinness Book of World Records* records the "Shortest Tap Dance" times.

I won that one, feet down.

27

The Ziegler hot dog factory tour

Rolling on the rotisserie in a theatre lobby, served out of a food cart near Times Square, or even being given away for a promotion of vinyl siding outside the Home Depot, we are overwhelmed by the slick, geasy, mustard and ketchup, delicious, sloppy memory of summer freedom: the hot dog. The quick, perfect sustenance. Vacation food in every sense.

There is a dark side, though, and that is how they are made.

My first year to teach, Selma, Alabama, 1967. Two years after the Edmund Pettus Bridge confrontations. A lot of tension. But I was oblivious to all of this. I was a first-year teacher. I was excited and scared witless. One hundred and fifty 12- 13 or slow 14-year olds floated out before me in a sea of desks, full of squirminess and awakening desires, both sexual and maniacal. In short, Junior High School.

Distraction, I decided; that was the key. A constant shell game. Find the hidden lesson plan that would work.

One of my colleagues had taught science for 750 years, was seasoned, wise and close to looney. Mrs. Reed. Her room looked like the last scene of *Raiders of the Lost Ark*. Dust was her friend. I almost expected a raven on the bust of Pallas over her door. I was afraid to look. But her key to engaging the students was field trips: Dallas County to find shark vertebrae sitting on top of little limestone columns eroded by the Alabama rains. Just pluck them up like bleached coins lost from Mesozoic galleons.

Or… touring the Ziegler Hot Dog Plant. Having already taken the shark vertebrae trip and hearing the kids squeal with discovery, I said, "Why not? Let's go to the Ziegler Hot Dog Plant!" Distraction. Out of the classroom. Away from prison. Enlightenment.

Slaughterhouse was about to enter our vocabulary. I was so excited about field trips that I studied for and got a commercial driver's license so I could drive the school bus. Save money. Look impressive, perched in what was the stiffest-steering mechanical yellow train car on rubber wheels. I had been a substitute bus driver my senior year in high school, so I felt at home in the monstrosity. One of my students's father worked at the meat packing plant, so all arrangements were made by Daddy for little Junior and his thirty closest friends.

A slaughterhouse. Thirty silly-putty kids, a naïve first-year teacher and a promised free coupon for a package of hot dogs at the local Piggly-Wiggly. The end would reward the means. What a learning experience.

A slaughterhouse.

The two tour guides met us in their white lab coats, Ziegler hard hats and grins straight out of a torture movie. After a brief lecture of cow-or-pig-to-hot-dog yumminess, we started the tour.

I thought it strange that we went back outside. Then stranger still that we went to the back of the plant to an animal corral, to an inclined ramp, walled in steel bars with a strange sledge hammer anchored to a rod suspended above the small opening.

A guide pushed a button

In the next minute, I aged ten years.

The sledge hammer swung into the small opening in a blur and made a complete circle back to its resting place. The children were fascinated. I aged another ten years.

I knew the law of inertia: the property of matter by which it retains its state of rest or its velocity along a straight line so long as it is not acted upon by an external force. Translation: Matter – a sledge hammer; external force – the forehead of a cow or pig. I was teaching physical science along with biology. How genius of me.

And then the animal arrived.

And then the faces changed.

It was too late. They already had their free coupons.

A strange thing happened to the air. There was not enough oxygen, just short of a vacuum, because 30 Junior High Students in a collective gasp sucked the air out of that part of Dallas County. The unsuspecting cow scrambled up the incline with the help of lab-coated cattle prodders. Its head was encased in an apparatus that seemed to just appear out of the side bars like giant steel crab pincers notched up to lightning speed.

There was a strange deafening after the impact. A silence that lasted as we, zombie, like – all walked back into the building having witnessed the end of innocence. I knew in my heart that

I had chosen the wrong profession. Instead of teaching all about life, I had brought 30 innocent humans to a public lynching, an electric chair execution. The rest of the tour would surely justify the need we humans have for food, sustenance and growth. Justification for murder. Please, God, surely.

The first room was vast, cold, open. Blood ran in troughs across the floor like dark red creeks on their way to the Red Sea. I thought of the streets of Jerusalem running red with infidel blood during the crusades. Somehow I didn't need to mention this allegory. One of the boys tugged silently at my sleeve, and as I turned to him, he pointed to the floor behind the group. Two girls had fainted. Laid out like chattel in a slaughterhouse. Like two innocents in a concentration camp. Stop. I give up. My memory is still FUBARed!

We got them to a "holding room." Lord knows why they had built it. Probably for wives or sissies to sit out the tour. I think many of the boys would have cherished being called a sissy just to wait out the Hot Dog Horror Ride at the Ziegler County Fair. But we were brave. We had free coupons.

We stepped over the little blood rivers on our way to the next room. Cow and pig heads which had been skinned were arranged on large wall pegs by their resident torture taxidermist. Some pegs were empty and bloody. The image is still seared.

I keep thinking of how many *Parrish High School, Selma 1* of those 30 kids are still in life-long therapy.

Some I'm sure are devout vegetarians. Probably all. Alas, the tour continued.

We were spared what I imagine was the meat hacking room of severed, dismembered, bloody carcasses. After the threat of more faintings, the tour guide opted to take us to the "vats of nasty-looking, grey pureed Shit Room." Big mix-master stainless steel bowls with beaters the size of Paul Bunyan's arms whirled the stinking grey pureed slop, as buckets of red dye were dumped into the gross maelstrom. The red dye. To make the hot dogs PINK.

The kids' eyes were so glazed over that they looked like the poster for *Children of the Damned*. Come to think of it, maybe they were.

The next room.

No one else had fainted. In fact the two weak-stomached girls had re-joined us. Their free coupons were clutched tightly in their little hands. Thank God they had missed the room with the severed heads. I was already thinking of who might know a good lawyer.

Having run the gamut from the sledge hammer to the mixing bowls of pink-dyed offal, the kids and I had lost the sensory connections to picnics, ball games, summer camp lunches we associated with the ubiquitous hot dog. We were lost in the wilderness, adrift at sea, trapped in a coalmine; all cliché nightmares rolled into a simple desire to see how a hot dog is made. With such a tragedy, there had to be some kind of comic relief. A satyr play at the end of *Medea*. My prayers were answered.

The last room.

I hadn't counted on satyr phalluses.

What looked like a giant metal cow's udder festooned with silver teats stood in the middle of the room. Connected to the silver teats were long condom-like skins, flaccidly draped along

long stainless steel tables which filled up the rest of the room. What innocence was left in these Keane-eyed children was about to evaporate.

The machine was turned on and all that pink gunk we had seen concocted in the previous room shot out of the giant steel teats and gorged all those innocuous skin tubes into the longest, stiffest, most unmistakenly erect 15-foot penises this side of Ancient Greece. Another loud, gasping intake of air by the boys rent the air. The girls were silent. Then the expected: Communal hysteria.

Laughter and body contortions never seen before. A riot of pointing and doubling-over. The boys had seen their first porn. The girls were still lost. I was embarrassingly amused but also knew my career was over. The tour guide had never seen this kind of reaction. He was lost. He flipped another switch and out of the tables arose robot arms that grasped the erections at six-inch intervals and tied off the end product. a string of hot dogs ready to be packaged, refrigerated and sent to local Piggly-Wiggly stores. Things we knew, treats we recognized, secrets we were privy to. Also prurient images better than a sex book under the covers with Daddy's flashlight.

When we got back on the bus, no one spoke. They were all gazing with blank stares out the bus window, scrambling all the images into something that held some kind of meaning. So was I.

My thoughts centered on lawsuits, post-traumatic stress syndrome and unemployment. The trip was never discussed in class after that day. It didn't happen. The feared repercussions never came. I seriously think there are 30 deep, dark secrets nestled way back in those now-adult brains, waiting to find their exorcism. I tell the story simply because it's true. And the truth will always set you free. And besides, I was the teacher. And the teacher always gets *two* free coupons.

At last Babylon

Summer 1968, free for three solid months from my first year of teaching, my friend Ed Norment and I took off for Hollywood in his VW "Sadie." "Sadie" was named after the Barbra Streisand song from *Funny Girl* – and it was apropos - we were going to Hollywood to meet her. How in hell we had no idea. And, we wanted to be on *The Dating Game*. But of longs shots, that one was the longest. Still how in hell. The only thing I remember about the trip out there was that Texas never ended. We stopped for no sightseeing as we had three days to get to L.A. We were going to meet up with two other college friends who also went out there in a VW, but earlier that week. We were going to stay with a guy who I vaguely knew through relatives of mine from Marengo County, Alabama. He was from Demopolis. I was from Putnam. Same county, but going to Dempolis was as distant as Greece or Rome. I had been to Demopolis probably two times in my life. So this guy was as much a stranger as Rock Hudson, but like Rock Hudson, he now lived in Hollywood. I was one degree of separation already. That's the naiveté that charted the map to fame.

We stacked on top of each other in his tiny apartment until we got our own short term lease place. It was the Argyle Apartments up the hill from the Capitol Records building. I had gone to heaven in a VW across Texas that never ended and so far no one had been at the Pearly Gates to say "sheep to the right, goats to the left." It only got better. The second night we were at… Dammit I just remembered his name: Buddy Ogletree! But he changed it to Buddy Galon out there. So the second night at Buddy's (he was a pianist for private parties) we all went to a Zodiac party. All twelve signs sat by each other in this big circle of fabulous chairs in the biggest house I'd ever been in. Buddy was at the baby grand and all four of us scattered around the room finding our signs. I'm Gemini and the only chair left was near an old lady seated in a Philadelphia wing back chair looking like a display at Madame Tussauds. I sat and she turned to me. "Who are you" she said. "Ronald Harris from Putnam, Alabama." I bleated out in what I'm sure sounded like Gomer Pyle at his stupidest. She took a minute to recover and then turned to me again and said, "Why are you here?" No pause, no shame, I told her I had come to Hollywood to meet Barbra Streisand and to be on *The Dating Game*. Without a beat she said, "I'll see what I can do." She took my phone number, which was Buddy's. I'd memorized it at my mother's request. I guess to use if I got lost and the police picked me up. I was 23, but my mother still thought I was 6. Thank you Mother. I was about to appreciate her wisdom even more. In two days, after we had moved into the Argyle which was furnished, not air conditioned, had a phone, I got a call from Buddy. The old lady had called, left her number and I was to call her. She had some news. The world that I lived in up to that moment was about to vaporize and in it's place would form, from that one phone call, into Babylon, the Milky Way, and somewhere near the end of where the Big Bang had slowed down a bit. She said, "Come to gate 10 at 20th Century Fox at 6am. Bring a dark suit, bring your three friends. You must each have a dark suit. You will all be extras in *Hello Dolly*. Don't be late. Your name will be at the gate. There are three days of

Me & Jerry - lunchbreak

work. You will get $50 a day. And write this down. On "such and such date" (I was numb by this time I was spinning into butter and wrote it down but can't of

145

course remember it now) you and your friends are to report to the ABC studios to audition for the *The Dating Game*." I had completely disappeared. I was traveling with Rod Taylor in *The Time Machine* and even the Morlocks were my friends. I was hearing God channeled through a 150 year (I was 23 and anyone over 50 looked mummified to me) old lady who sat next to me in a Philadelphia wing back chair that I didn't realize at the time was His throne and I was the chosen sheep that was about to get one of His mansions. Oh yeah, I didn't tell you her name. She was Buster Keaton's sister-in-law, Constance Tallmadge, sister to Norma and Natalie (Buster Keaton's wife) and was in D.W.Griffiths *Intolerance*. Now, I

On the set for Hello Dolly

know her footprints are at Grauman's Chinese Theatre and her star in the Hollywood Walk of Fame is at 6300 Hollywood Blvd. I'm 63 (I wrote this in 2008) and I graduated from high school in 1963. The planets continued to line up as I tell this story.

Babs and I.

We all piled into one of the VW's and got to 20th Century Fox to find there were three thousand of us extras. Sure enough my name was on a huge list: "Ronald Harris and three friends."

146

We were herded off towards long covered tables with hats: bowlers, boaters, toppers; shirts with high collars; ties; shoes to go with our dark suits. This was the 60s so suits were 3 buttons with narrow lapels which wasn't far from the dark suit coats of the 1890s. As we moved in single file past all these costumers, we would yell out our hat size, get thrown a hat – I got a terrific black bowler, my friend Jerry got a straw boater. One of my favorite pictures in my house are us in 1890s costumes eating lunch on the *Peyton Place* set. We're sitting on an overturned boat in front of Harrington Bros. Motorcycle Inc. There's snow everywhere. It's really only salt. The temperature those three days were in the high 90s. That snow never melted. I didn't even realize it was hot. I was in paradise. There were so many extras that we were in layers along the street. The scene was the big parade when Streisand sings, "Before the Parade Passes By." We were called wavers. Way back behind the real extras that belonged to the Screen Extras Guild. They didn't have to bring their suits. They were dressed in resplendent grandeur. They were the ones in the close ups and next to the curb. We just waved, way back there in Blursville. I didn't care. I was going to see Barbra Streisand and certain to meet her and become fast friends. I mean why not, I'd been in Hollywood a week and was already in a movie! Not to mention soon to be a TV star.

Lunch was a circus. What seemed like a convoy of white catering trucks would pull up to this immense parking lot and all of us, all 3000, would mass towards them. The truck backs would roll up and the caterers would toss white boxes at the 6000 upheld hands. It was a food relief scene from a third world country. The country of Make Believe on the continent of Dreamland. One day it was lunch on the *Peyton Place* set, the next on *The War Lord* set, and the third and last day we all four ate in Perry Mason's courtroom. An acid trip could not have been weirder. And I was being paid to boot. And there was Streisand. Oh and I forgot – my director was Gene Kelly. A wet dream with sunlight in Technicolor.

Ok, so one afternoon after waving for hours on end as the 27 floats and bands and unicyclists and Clydesdales and Civil War veteran and suffragettes and gymnasts and God knows what's passed by take after take after take… there was this sudden calm. All the action stopped. Mr. Kelly told us over his bull horn as he was sitting way up in a boom camera truck that a close-up was to be set up. Up until this there had been no Barbra. I had shamelessly gone to her trailer on two breaks with a picture of her I wanted autographed. Her maid would answer the knock and say "Miss Streisand is not available." I now realized out of the 3000 people there I was the only stalker. Why I wasn't kicked off the set never occurred to me. After all everything I had wished for had come true. Why not chat with Babs? I looked great in my costume. She had no choice but to love me, even though she was 25 and I was 23. During the set up for the close-up, the 1st assistant director asked over his bullhorn for all the extras who wanted to be in the shot to stand close to the curb. Many didn't give a rat's ass about standing in the 95 degree heat for hours for the set up and take after take, so only, say 1000, stood on the curb. He walked passed us and pointed out those he liked. We all four were standing there grinning like dolts and he stopped, and in what I remember as extreme slow motion, his arm raised with that "God as my co-pilot" finger and pointed at… me. My grin extended off the edges of my face and I felt the same feeling I had when I had rededicated my life to Jesus during a summer revival. All floaty and heady when you dream you are flying. Lifting up in front of your friends and just doing loop-the-loops out over a corn field with Disney birds as your companions, with wings on your feet like Mercury, all naked and fully clothed at the same time. Christmas morning and you get your first train.

My three friends wanted nothing to do with me for the rest of the day. I didn't care, I was getting to be in a close up with Barbra. I was homecoming King and I was just voted Most Popular. They just didn't want it bad enough. I had even prayed to God to let it be me. And He answered my prayer. He answered it with that finger in slow motion choosing me from the masses and I moved with the chosen to a spot where she was going to be. And my life was complete at 23.

And there she was. Her entourage: a man with a stool that placed it under her Oscar winning tush wherever she desired to rest (she never looked at him, he just knew); two makeup people with portable battery fans to cool her make up (it was 95 degrees); a big bruiser who walked around in a cruciform position protecting her from horses, floats, camera equipment, and stalkers; a seamstress constantly repairing the hem of her costume; a lady holding her feather boa (I innocently asked if I could touch it and she snapped back, "No. Each of these feathers are numbered!" I slinked away like a beaten dog); the cinematographer, Harry Straddling, Sr. and all his crew; Gene Kelly; 1st, 2nd assistant directors; and a few chosen for the close-up. I couldn't feel the fake cobble stone street I was standing on. I had levitated about six inches from the 20th century Fox back lot. The only thing that came to mind was "He is not here. He is risen."

The shot was set up. I was to stand behind the lady with the umbrella. Streisand was about four feet from me. During the "cuts" I would nonchalantly glance in her direction. We locked eyes for 2 nanoseconds and I instantly became myself in my nightmare where I'm only in my underwear and it's some crowded Greyhound bus station somewhere in the Midwest, I know no one, have no ticket, and an erection. The worst thing is that no one notices me. When she turned away I suddenly felt so lost. She didn't recognize me. I was no one. It took a while for my clothes to materialize and to this day I still occasionally have that same nightmare. She's always walking away from me and the woman with the feather boa is mouthing something vile in my direction. Such is perpetual disappointment visualized in night time sub-consciousness. I have this fantasy feeling I'll meet her one day and when I tell her this tale she will look at me for more than 2 nanoseconds and say "I thought I recognized you, but wasn't sure." She'll say, "Weren't you the one that came to my trailer with my picture? Yes, now I remember. Thank you for being my number 1 fan. You make me young!" Okay so I get a little carried away…

After the closeup (which by the way they reshot the next day and I was not chosen, and my friends reveled in my fall from grace), they filmed the dialogue between the actress playing Ernestina Simple, a hoochi coochie girl on a meat packers float, as the set up date for Horace Vandergelder which Dolly knows will end in disaster and Horace will end up in her arms. When you watch this scene the piglets in the girls' arms on the float are laid back, tongues hanging out, and comatose. Not very natural for piglets. Here's the skinny on the piglets in Hollywoodland.

Each had a Humane Society trainer (five piglets, five men in white lab coats) that stood guard. When the 1st assistant director would shout "Background," the five would approach the piglets squealing their little nuts off, grab them gently by their back legs, place them kind of rock-a-by in their other hand and all in unison, at the count of three, swing them 360 degrees for about 5 rotations, getting the little fockers drunk as skunks. With their tongues hanging out, the trainers gave them back to the actresses on the float. "Action", dialogue, pigs wake up, barnyard hell,

"Cut", more swinging 360 degrees, back to actresses, "Action," dialogue… all afternoon in that 95 degree heat. All for the sake of a visual in the background of a character in a movie musical. Or was it Streisand wanting no distractions? Or was it 20th Century Fox going bankrupt as the millions ticked by?

Whatever I had imagined of glamour and the movies up to that point had suddenly given way to nothing more than training your dog not to pee on the carpet or hump your leg. Movie Stars are just people like us, but with attendants to hold stools, boas, and fans to cool their beauty, their armpits, their jets. Yep. Just like us except no one volunteered to rehem my pants at the end of the day in the country of Make Believe on the continent of Dreamland.

When I watch that scene in the movie, I can catch a fleeting glimpse of a man in a black bowler hat waving it to some stranger passing in formation with a thousand other feet marching to a prerecorded sound track, on a fake street, with fake store fronts, toward some kind of happiness.

At least I think that's me.

29

The Dating Game

Ilost. But damn, it was close to the most magical thing that's ever happened to me. Already on the biggest high from the *Hello, Dolly!* experience, I reported to ABC studios. We, my three friends and I, and about 100 other guys, were taken to a room with dividers lined up in the center from one end to the other. On both sides of this seven foot tall barricade were 100 chairs. Girls on one side, guys on the other. We were all given numbers, one to 100. Girls and guys couldn't see each other–we were just numbers. I was dressed to the tens. I thought we'd meet the girls. Loopy me.

I forgot what my number was. Let's say 23. So soon, this wacked out guy who called out the numbers, sort of like the old Roman claques that jazzed up the audience before a show with jokes and general nuttiness, said "Beautiful lady #15, ask handsome guy, #23 a question." We had been advised to be provocative (I had no idea in Hell what that meant.), but not vulgar (that I knew), sexy but not sexual (that really confused this country boy). So #15 girl (and this was her actual question) called out over the wall to me, "Number 23, if you're taking me to a fancy restaurant, I want you to sing the menu to me. You know what my favorite food is!" Without a beat I was so damn nervous the first thing that popped in my cornbread-fed brain was a line from the musical *Oklahoma!* that I had been in during college. I warbled, "Gonna give you barley, carrots and pertaters, pasture for the cattle, spinach and termaters...." "How about that?" I said with glee.

The Dating Game 1968

Another one of those quantum hiccups happened in that room. The molecules in front of everyone's face changed from natural neutron, electron, and proton arrangement to some subatomic melee caused by the nuclear collision of country twang, blatant

153

idiocy and unbridled caterwauling. After one second of "pin drop," the room exploded into what I thought was "laughing with" but was, I am sure, "laughing at." But I had my first large captive audience. And boy did I turn up the hick-o-meter. I got only one other question, something about Crayola Crayons, and the wildest thing happened. All the guys leaned forward or backwards in their chairs to stare at me. Jethro Bodean's idiot brother had escaped the attic, somehow managed to steal a suit, get a number and crashed ABC studios. What in God's name would he say next! I only heard "crayon" from her because of the open jawed gawkers riveted on me. With a sudden jolt of spotlight mania, I told her that, "the copper one was my favorite and that I used it last..." Then, in the headiness of celebrity I told one of my biggest secrets...I told the entire room that, not only was it used last, but that when no one was looking at me in my grammar school class that... I ate it... paper and all 'cause I didn't want anyone else to have it. I had a severe pathological issue that I was sharing now with 200 of the most beautiful people on the planet who were witnessing certifiable two digit intelligence coming out of the mouth of a moron. What a prize date! Needless to say, I got no more questions.

Well the guys levitated out of the fiberglass bucket chairs and the cacophony of hysteria wafted over the room in layers of both ridiculous and sublime ridicule. I didn't care. I was the center of the universe. Lord only knows how the girls were reacting. But I imagined them all raring back their Aquanet helmet heads and swooning over my brilliance.

My fame was sealed when the claque called out 25 guy numbers and 25 girl numbers and the rest could go home. Home to Shameville, USA. By God if they didn't call three of us four guys' numbers. When I heard "23," the stone rolled away and He arose. Poor Ed had to endure our hysteria, his number was not called, but he wasn't into girls anyway. He played the organ.

We lined up to sign some agreement that I thought was for an appearance the next day. When the guy took all our stats and said, "We'll call in two weeks to two months." Panic struck me. We would be gone back to Alabama before we had our fifteen–actually 30 minutes of fame. I blurted out "We're going home next week! We've got to be on TV NOW!" I was lying through my Southern teeth, but some planets, probably outer ones, lined up and he did the proverbial eye roll and said he'd see what he could do. He did.

That next week we taped the shows. All three of us were on separate shows. Days apart. How much of our Southern accents could America take day after day? I was grouped with a guy from England who had a strong brogue and smelled like he had used cow shit for cologne. A guy from the Midwest with no accent, and of course me filling out the Triumvirate as Goober from Mayberry. Well you can guess their reasoning. I just wish I had been seated away from the rank smelling Brit, but other than that I was about to enter that shiny floor world of garish flower backdrops and eternal fame. They taped five shows a day so we sat in the Green Room watching the boobs asking the goobs questions that made no frickin' sense to me. But I had it down pat: sexy not sexual, provocative not vulgar, clever not stupid. I was a little in denial about the last one. I had finally conquered my nerves as we sat there in the three chairs on the turntable ready to spin into infamy, when all of a sudden the claque gets in my face and whispers, with a jackass-eating-briars grin, "Just remember, only 80 MILLION PEOPLE ARE WATCHING YOU TODAY! SMILE!"

The butterflies I had partially collected and pinned to the inside of my stomach ripped out of their javelined guts and started feeding on my psyche. I thought I was about to vomit.

We swung around and there it was... Ringling Brothers, Barnum and Bailey with Jim Lange as Ringmaster. The audience was animated to the point of prelaunch. The music was so familiar it seemed like the world had turned out just for me. It was Birthday, Christmas and Vacation Bible School in my head. The butterflies all died, their manic wings dissolving into my gastric juices. I was alone in a spotlight when they announced, "Bachelor Number 3 is Ronald Harris from Alabama." The room spun away, the tall director's chair I was seated in began to orbit the sun in a slow warm arc that felt as good as sleep and as euphoric as the day I climbed over the wooden fence to the barn and my genitals banged together in perfect alignment and I had my first boy "spasm". What brought me back was the Midwest guy poking me. They were asking me to say "Hello" to the girl. Since I had just had an orbit around the sun, I had not heard her name. I leaned into his space and said, "What's her name?" Of course I was miked so the first thing out of my mouth was "Tobacco Road" mixed with HeeHaw with a bit of brain damage from a tractor wreck thrown in. I was out of the gate and falling flat on my face. But that same thing that happened in the preliminary room happened again. Gales of laughter from the peanut galleries as Mr. Midwest told me her name and I said, "Hello so and so." It was as if I had paid them one hundred dollars each to goad me on. And when I looked at Jim Lange and saw his head upturned in laughter. I was ON!

Her first question to me was "I'm crossing the desert with you in a covered wagon. What luxuries would you have for me?" Provocative not vulgar, sexy not sexual being my mantra I, without a second thought said, "Well the first thing I would do is have installed... an indoor toilet." Not "bathroom" or "powder room" or other euphemisms for shit hole! I pronounced "toilet" to the world in probably the longest verbalization of a two syllable word ever filmed. The live laugh tracks grew louder and I took on the power of oneness that had nothing to do with getting a date or saving whatever reputation I had up to that moment. Shoot, I was smoking rabbit tobacco with Billy Earl and getting higher than buzzards circling over a dead horse. I guess the girl was responding to her Christian duty involved with hiring the handicapped, so I got one more question. "Bachelor Number Three, I'm lying on a towel down by the ocean. You come along. Where is the first place you would kiss me?" Feigning the idea of traveling down her body to pick a "sexy but not sexual" place, I cocked my eyes up to the right as if I was traveling down into her "hills and valleys" and after "careful" thought said, "on the...BEACH!" I had seen the movie *On the Beach* at the Thomasville Theatre in 1959 and its impact obviously was hidden away just for this stellar moment. The pauses before each word I'd learned from the other guys, like set ups to something nasty. Well I nailed the timing and without any thought about metaphors or "sounds like" or genuine cleverness... remember every two syllable word I spoke stretched into infinity... beach gave way to "Beeeee...acha." The first thing that happened as the din rose , was the cameraman right in front of me dropped to his knees in hysterics or like he was having a stroke. A shot of heroin, a gold, good conduct star, an A+ in Class Clown all were given to me at that moment. I was cooking with gas, no more wood burning stove for me.

I looked at Jim Lange who was bent over laughing. Me thinking it was "with me" not "at me." So I grinned the claque's jackass in a cactus patch grin.

She chose the Midwest guy as probably the only one who spoke a language she understood. I was hoping if I lost she'd get the "Eau de Cowshit" guy, but no such luck. And who gives a crap about winning a weekend in Flagstaff, Arizona at the

Holiday Inn with a chaperone! That was the "expense paid trip to a fun locale." I got three Janzen mock turtlenecked, short-sleeved, striped knit shirts. Valued at about 10 bucks for all three. Whoop-de-doo! But as proof of that day in Bozoland, I still have 2 of them. I wore a size "medium" then. A size 40 coat and 32-32 pants and on that day I was perfect in all ways. She just didn't know how I could have changed her into a princess at the Holiday Inn in Flagstaff, AZ. I would have been glad to bring the dresses. I had several.

From the taping in June to August 9, 1968, when the episode aired, I let the world that I knew know about my fame. I sent postcards to every kid I had taught my first year. After all I was going to be their teacher in September. They were the luckiest students on the planet. A teacher who had been on *The Dating Game* and in *Hello, Dolly!* A star who chose to come back to Selma, Alabama, and teach them Biology. Giving up a stellar career on TV and in the movies just to teach them frog dissection and mitosis. They were honored to be in the presence of a T.V. Christian martyr.

I was in Putnam with my parents that August, and the only channel out that far in the country they could get was CBS. So we all dressed up: my Mama, Daddy and best friend, Melanie Hamilton. We headed off to Meridian, Mississippi, the nearest "big city" to their Sears store. Meridian is 55 miles from Putnam. I knew I was too special to watch on just one TV set. We went in Sears, I approached the TV salesman with great pride, "Sir, I'm going to be on *The Dating Game* today. Can I turn on one of your TVs to the ABC channel?" Seeing the four of us standing there all dolled up, he probably was thinking this was the only trip they allowed for their pinhead son, so he gently patronized me with this statement, "How can you be on TV today son, you're here with me?" Being treated as a simpleton when I was to be so famous brought out my ire, but being with God-fearing parents and my best friend, I stifled my rage and calmly told him that I had been in Hollywood in June and that we had taped the show. He shrugged his Dacron wash-and-wear, cheap Sears suit shoulders, turned on one TV set and walked away. He stood at a safe distance from the family that got only one channel and probably ran a seedy fish camp down by the Tombigbee River. We stood there bunched together as if it was a photo set-up for Olan Mills. I saw all these other blank TVs, 26 in all, reflecting us. The joy of me on 26 TVs gave me such power that, without asking, I turned them all on and switched each to ABC. It felt like NASA headquarters, 1962, and John Glenn was on the wall of monitors. Ronald Harris was orbiting around the earth on 18" capsules stacked in perfect rows, brand spanking new and all about to belong to me.

The theme music started, Jim Lange in his big coaster size, wire-rimmed glasses did his overblown intro, and then the set turned to great applause. We were each described in our chairs in the dark and when my intro was over I was shaking so badly I almost peed on myself. That day in Sears, I was wearing the same outfit that I had taped in, navy blue with burgundy stripe, double-breasted jacket and navy pants, white shirt, burgundy tie. When the lights came up on me on my TV stool, I couldn't breathe. Mama and Daddy realized I had not been lying all summer and Melanie hugged me. Then I started breathing again. The salesman came running over, looked at the TV, looked at me, looked back at the TV and burst out, in his best salesman voice turned up to maximum volume, "Goddamn… that is you!" He became a wild man. Yelling for all the clerks to come see a real live TV person. Cash registers all over the store were abandoned. No telling how much money was stolen from

Sears that infamous day of abandoned cash registers. Customers massed around us like visitors to the zoo. They'd look at me, look at the TV, and look back at me. It was scary, fabulous and weird. Helium mixed with nitrous oxide. And when I heard my first answer and it was so damn stupid and so lame, I suddenly felt like I was in the *Hello, Dolly!* nightmare: underwear, bus station, lost in the Midwest, no ticket, but this time no erection. This time I had no penis and to top it all off, there was a big hole in the front of my underwear. Everyone was laughing and pointing. Even the woman holding Barbra's feather boa. She was knee slapping hysterical.

The rest of the TV show was woozy. The camera would cut to the bachelorette's face when I answered. Her reaction was disgust mixed with fear. I've never seen such pie plate eyes on a human female face. No wonder I lost. I was the missing link, painting leaping mules on a cave somewhere in lower Alabama and eating raw possum meat. When she came around to hug us, I realized for the first time as I watched why she had barely touched me in the hug. Now I know why she didn't want to touch a troglodyte. I watched her hug the cowshit guy and he didn't bother her. Well she was a floozy anyway. Her skirt was up to her coochie and her make-up was designed by someone from Babylon via Sodom and Gomorrah. Mama and Daddy wouldn't have wanted me to go to Flagstaff, AZ with a Jezebel. Chaperone or not.

I vaguely remember answering some curious customer questions about how I got chosen, but since I lost there wasn't much reason for them to fawn over a loser. "Ahh fame, thou fleeting bauble," as Captain Hook says in *Peter Pan*. But I was a star in my students' eyes, and the next year was one of the best of the 40 years I taught. They were young, impressionable and kind. I fell in love with all 150 of them. And they learned how to dissect frogs and all about mitosis. I won in their minds. They even liked the shirts I won. I wore them on field trips. I never told them I thought the bachelorette was just plain white trailer trash.

California Dreamin'

Geraldine Page & Me

*T*here is no greater tour de force of acting to me, than Geraldine Page in *Sweet Bird of Youth* as Alexandra Del Lago accepting Walter Winchell's accolades over the phone for her cinematic comeback while she carries on a scathing rejection of Paul Newman's Chance Wayne pleading to be mentioned as an up and coming leading man.

As Miss Page fawns and mews and transports herself into that rarified world of ego and selfish tragic dependence on fame, she literally kicks the most beautiful man on the planet out of her bed and figuratively out of her life. That one cinematic scene is the definition of the massive difference between fame and artistry, and Miss Page was doing both at the same time. At the time I saw it in the early 60s, I was so over saturated with her talents and looks and bravery, I couldn't imagine her being anyone else. Her Alexandra Del Lago was completely real and completely a fading star. Geraldine Page didn't exist. That how movies fried my brain. I was 18 and movies were more than suspensions of disbelief.

I was home for the holidays in 1966, and another seminal moment of acting occurred. I was watching, for the first time, Truman Capote's A Christmas Memory and having missed the opening credits, I sat transfixed until the end waiting to see who this incredible actress playing Capote's old cousin Miss Sook Faulk was. Of course at the end of the telecast I was relating to my own childhood because Capote's story takes place 75 miles from Putnam in Monroeville and was filmed in Alabama. The credits rolled. My God. It couldn't be. How, in only four years, could the elegant and evil Alexandra Del Lago become the broken, childlike heap of humanity of Miss Sook Faulk?

When I was in New York in the spring of 1983, I saw Miss Page as mother superior in Agnes of God, another breathtaking performance. After the show, shamelessly waiting for her autograph, I tried to find words to say to her. I'd remembered how her line in A Christmas Memory, "I could leave the world with today in my eyes" had broken my heart. If I could say it to her without falling apart, I would try. As she graciously signed my Playbill I said, "Miss Page, you've spoken my favorite line in all of literature: 'I could leave the world with today in my eyes.'" She stopped her signing of another fan's Playbill and looked at me. Angels sang when she said, "That's my favorite also. Are you from the South?"

What followed from that night on was a trajectory so clean and pure that it still blazes with clarity and details.

We wrote each other, she sent me an autographed picture, and

I saw two more of her performances with her Mirror Repertory Company at St. Peter's Church: W. Somerset Maugham's *Rain* in 1984 and his *The Circle* in 1986. It's the night I saw *The Circle* that's most memorable.

I got on the elevator to go up to the second floor where the theatre space was. Getting on with me were two other playgoers and a pitiful "bag lady" with a knit toboggan pulled way down to her eyebrows, two huge bags in her hands, and what seem like two or three coats. In my pocket was a letter from Miss Page to see her after the show. The elevator stopped on the second floor and the two patrons stepped out. I motioned for the "bag lady" to go before me, but she put the bags down, pushed the button for the third floor and then looked at me. She lifted the toboggan up a bit and smiled. It was Miss Page incognito going up to her dressing room on the third floor. I can't even begin to describe how I felt. I'll just say I laughed after she did and offered to take her bags when the door opened. She said to follow her. She entered a very small dressing room, motioned for me to sit and as she sat in front of her tiny mirror she removed the knit hat and underneath was a wig cap over her pressed down hair. She began to chat. I began to breathe. Miss Page took off her coat and underneath was a smock-like black dress. She reached for what looked like yards and yards of dark, swirly, red and black fabric hanging nearby, she stepped behind a screen (still chatting about the repertory company, my life, her life) and stepped back out in this miraculous caftan that was her costume for the opening of *The Circle*. I was still having difficulty breathing. She sat, reached for her wig and proceeded with a routine that transformed this magnificent chameleon from a shadow in the elevator to a fully illuminated grand dame. She turned to me and touched my hand, "I hope you love the show." That was my exit line.

I don't actually remember much about the plot of the show. I had been anesthetized by absolute artistry. The journey, both physical and mental, from elevator to hand pat, the access to one of the greatest actresses of the 20th century, the viewing of her latest performance redefined the craft of acting. It's almost like I read about this sequence of events somewhere long ago and somehow wished it into my own memory. But it was me, it was her and it was how I described it.

On Oscar night in 1986 when Geraldine Page's name was called for best actress for *The Trip to Bountiful* and the camera panned to her, she finally stood (We found out later that she was trying to put her shoes back on because her feet hurt and she and everyone thought it would go to Meryl Streep for *Out of Africa*), she started forward to the stage, kissing friends along the way. And then I realized I had seen her dress before.

She was wearing her costume from *The Circle*. She had

touched my hand while wearing that caftan. And in her acceptance speech she mentioned The Mirror Repertory Company. That was the proof. That night in her dressing room had actually happened. After seven nominations she finally won her Oscar. I felt one degree of separation when F. Murray Abraham opened the envelope and said: "I consider her to be the greatest actress of the English language… Geraldine Page!" I knew that already. But her even greater fluency was how she mastered the unspoken language of the human heart.

31

Pearl & the deer heart

Pearl was the last of the black ladies to help my Mama around the place. There had been Granny (Junior's Mama), Maryetta and Margaret (mother and daughter) before Pearl. All the way from the 50s until the early 90s, Mama had been blessed with these black women who were her helpers, confidants and friends. Because of my mother's upbringing in the rural Jim Crow South, my Mama never would address the issue of friendship. They were "the help." But we knew without them she would have been very lonely there on Highway 69, miles from neighbors her age.

Mama loved her world there in our one and half story white clapboard house with its two big live oaks in the front yard and acres and acres of pasture land stretching to a pine and sweet gum horizon way back behind the house. Mama hardly ever sat down to do anything but work; cutting up a boiled chicken for her famous chicken salad (we still have her black handle scissors she fancied to dice the meat), washing turnip greens out on the back porch in a cane bottom chair straddling a number one washtub; or her favorite sit down chore; shelling peas, butterbeans, or snapping beans. All the things I hated to do.

To Mama it meant sustenance for the winter, not just a present day meal, something to freeze or can "in case" there was, God knows what, the end of the world. As I've mentioned before Mama and Daddy married during the Great Depression and practically lived off the truck farm products of the garden behind the house or government commodities, so the present was just enough time to get everything ready for the end of the world.

We shelled a lot of peas.

But the one day Pearl was there with me and Mama, sitting out on our carport in those aluminum green and white latticed lawn chairs somewhere in the middle of a summer justified all the pea shelling I had done up until then. A revelation was about to come from Pearl that would chill that sweltering air lying around us like the inside of an August cotton house at sundown.

"Miss Helen?" Pearl finally spoke after Mama asked her why she was so quiet. "Miss Helen, they tried to kill me last night."

I perked up.

Mama stopped shelling. "Who?" she asked with some alarm, and Pearl told us.

Pearl had heard a commotion out in her backyard that woke her up. Out there in the dark she could make out two people digging a hole in the corner of her back yard, just inside her property that joined her neighbor's. She said she knew right off what they were doing. And it was for revenge. Seems that Pearl had grown tired of dope being brought up from Mobile by a certain dealer. She had threatened to go to the authorities because they were dealing drugs next door, and she was a God fearing woman who knew that they were doing sinful things among the young people she helped raise. She knew

what they were burying, and she knew she had to dig it up before sunrise.

Pearl said she stayed in the shadows of her porch and waited. The intruders finally left and she waited a few more minutes. Waiting too long would cause her to die. Slouching out across her yard with no moon and only a distant vapor mercury streetlight to help her find the fresh grave, she crawled the last few feet, patting the ground to find the new turned dirt. She found it and began to claw at it as she felt her life slowly leaving her body. She prayed to Jesus that she was not too late.

She found it.

It was not too late.

Covered in dirt, sticking to its slimy peritoneum, was a deer's heart.

It was still beating.

She knew when it stopped she would die.

Pearl told Mama and me something about "hoo-doo." How bad people use a beating deer heart buried in the corner of their victim's yard at night to kill, to hoo-doo, their enemy. She believed in it. She was as Christian as my Mama, but put a deer heart out somewhere near her zinnias or camellia bush and it stops beating? Death. Hoo-doo death. Not a peaceful death.

Pearl knew differently. Pearl knew you would die violently. Suddenly bolting upright in your bed as the last breath flew out of your mouth in a silent scream.

Nobody dies peacefully.

Somewhere, somehow, evil is involved. In the Bible it was a snake. In Pearl's yard it was Bambi's heart under a hoo-doo spell.

Mama's expression never changed as I lost feeling in my hands. Were they in the pan of peas? Floating above me? Not even connected to my arms? I was dumbfounded, flabbergasted, discombobulated – all the polysyllable words for "Damn!"

Damn, what a story!

Deer heart still beating, buried in your yard.

My God, my degree in Biology was just negated, along with my entire Christian upbringing. Suddenly I realized Pearl had stopped the story just as she pulled the thing from the ground. Good Lord, was it still beating? Is it in her purse next to her chair? Have mercy, what would I do if she said it was still beating there on her dining room table, on a platter she washed just for the occasion?

I looked at Mama who calmly went back to shelling. There was this silence as thick as the sauna bath air around us. I felt like I was breathing chewing gum.

I came back to earth slightly when Pearl said the heart had kept beating until the sun was up. Then it stopped. She was safe. She made it through the hoo-doo.

The afternoon blurred by and when Pearl had gone, I asked Mama what had just happened. Deer hearts don't beat when ripped from bodies, at least not after being slammed in a hole of dirt, rescued, and watched closely 'til sunrise.

"Mama, please tell me you don't believe that story."

My Mama, going through her shelled peas and picking out the dark, shriveled, faulty ones and tossing them in with all the hulls down by her side, said in the voice of a priest, "Son, she believes it."

32

Miss Willie Downey

Daddy found her dead of a massive stroke on October 1st, 2001. He had gone to pick her up for church that Sunday morning like he had done for many years since my Mama died. She was dressed in her best, lying face up on her bed. She probably had felt bad, sat on the edge of the bed, and there inside her skull something exploded and she fell back onto the double-wedding ring quilt she fancied. Miss Willie lived neat and tidy, and died the same way.

Her purse was on the bed beside her. It held her "widow's mite." Just enough money for her ticket to Heaven. She always dressed up when she traveled. And that day was no different. My Mama had an estranged friendship with Miss Willie. They were typical "coffee and pie" friends, but there was a distance. An incident from the 60s never was completely forgotten by my Mama. Postmasters and Postmistresses were politically appointed since the Federal government totally ran the postal service then. Miss Willie was Putnam's Postmistress for many years. She was a Republican. Then the Democrats came into power.

Daddy and Mama were "yellow dog" Democrats, and Mama was appointed to run the post office. For 8 years – as long as we had Democrats in control of state politics, Mama was Postmistress. Daddy and Mama were the last of the New Deal generation. They were the most conservative Democrats that ever lived. They had to be, they owed it to FDR.

So when the political climate changed back in Alabama, so did the post office bosses. My Mama lost her job back to the Republicans. Mama never really talked about it, but Miss Willie didn't eat as much pie in our house as she used to. Things came around gradually as Miss Willie began to lose her family. Her husband, Alba, had already died before she "got" the Post Office back, and then one by one she lost her children. Ray, her oldest son, died of a heart attack. Her daughter Marilyn died of a stroke. Eldred, the middle son, was cutting grass and his heart stopped. Her only son left was Harold. He lived in Mobile, 125 miles away. So Miss Willie was totally alone. My Mama's heart warmed and over the years, until she died in 1994, she started saving the last piece of pie. Whenever we had holiday gatherings we went and got Miss Willie. She was a diabetic, no sugar allowed; she even gave herself shots. My Mama's pies redefined "sweet," but somehow Miss Willie gobbled away. You can will yourself away from your troubles if the medicine is redemption served on holiday china.

On my way back to Huntsville after visiting my folks in the

80s and 90s I would always stop by to tell Miss Willie good-bye, and that I loved her. We talked of her gladiolas or her pitcher collection. (There was a chock-o-block frieze circling her dining room near the ceiling – shelf after shelf of over 100 pitchers, given, collected, bargained for, or swapped out. All different, all sparking clean, all worth practically nothing – except to Miss Willie. They were her new "children," her hobby distracting her from profound loss.) I sometimes would cut weeds, or if I had not seen her for a long time, would take her hedge clippers and trim out unwanted mimosa saplings that had invaded her flower beds. She had, in

Miss Willie's house present day

the last few years, gone almost completely blind. A county Home Health lady would come to teach her how to cook "blind." Miss Willie knew literally every square inch of her kitchen. She had lived in it for 50 or 60 years. The blind cooking was just a minor inconvenience. She still "read" her Bible every day with a magnifying glass thick enough to focus the sun and burn down the big oaks in the front yard. But there was one day I stopped by that was right up there with seeing the Blue Mosque in Istanbul or a total eclipse of the sun in Egypt.

When I got there she was not on her front porch as she always was after I would phone to tell her I was stopping by. I knocked, and because she was also almost deaf, I got no response. I knocked louder and finally heard her call out, "Come on in, Ronald, I'm in the bedroom!" I remember everything about that day with such clarity. The smell of her house was always the usual shut-away, no air conditioning, oldness – of layer and layers of thick Stanley furniture polish on tables and chairs, carved by hand from trees felled by her relatives from the 1800s. But that day, there was something a little off the norm, a kind of organic sweetness, almost like a cake in the oven. I knocked on her half-open bedroom door, "Miss Willie?" "I'm in here. Come help me." There was no panic in her voice.

I entered the room. Nothing made sense. There were all her cooking pots, boilers, saucepans, mixing bowls, even a Tupperware lettuce crisper (remember those sea foam green ones in everyone's refrigerators?) scattered all over the room; on the bed, the mantle, the dresser, the top of the chiffarobe, the night stand. She was moving them slightly to the right or left. And then I heard what was causing her urgency.

Drips. Drops of something were falling from out of her ceiling into the pots and pans. It wasn't raining that day, and no one lived upstairs on the second floor of her house. There had never been plumbing up there so no water leaks. She looked at me, smiling as she shifted a layer-cake pan near her pillow on the bed and said, "The bees came back! Help me with the honey!"

Honey was falling out of the cracks in her plaster ceiling! Yes, honey! As we replaced half full containers with empty ones, she exclaimed with great joy how it had been years since the bees had built their hives between her ceiling and the sub-flooring upstairs; that they had come in where a few bricks had broken away from the outside chimney and found their home again. Standing there, in her high ceiling bedroom, while around me rained white Dutch clover honey into mismatched kitchen ware, I felt her joy wash over me. As she scurried about, moving the cake-baking air, she turned a room that had always held loneliness into a rainforest unique to her world. She painted for me a scene both unnatural and as common as your everyday chores, one that rivaled Magritte's Granny Smith apple heads or Dali's melting watches.

She looked at me and said nonchalantly, as she dipped a finger into the pan at the foot of her bed, "Manna from Heaven! Wanna taste?"

My Daddy: Mr. Willard

Daddy lived for eight years after Mama died. He was in the last treatments of chemo when she left us. My sisters and I had doubts he would make it through the terrible weakness that seemed to dissolve the rebar that had always held his concrete being upright and stronger than an oxen he had plowed with when he and Mama were first married. Daddy still wore the same size clothes as he had then. He never gained weight because he worked constantly, driven by the same fear Mama had that there might never be enough. In March of 2002, he met that old man's companion pneumonia and went to be with Mama. He never had learned to cook so we worried he would just slowly disappear into loneliness and neglect.

Well, we were wrong. Daddy certainly knew how to open cans. The can opener was his weapon of choice against the war of living alone. My sisters checked up on him every day and saw him often. I got home when I could, but he didn't want to be pampered. His routine remained the same. Find something to do, fix whatever looked like it might break, visit

My Daddy, Mr. Willard

whoever needed cheering up, and never miss church on Sundays. He was a deacon and treasurer in the Putnam Baptist Church for 50 years.

During the Great Depression, he ran government salt pork, sugar and flour from Montgomery back to Marengo County where his destitute neighbors and other county residents that were once strangers lived. Everyone knew Mr. Willard and throughout his life he amazed us with his familiarity with "so and so" and "he had a brother named..."

He went through phases of rearing all kinds of farm animals.

Cows were his passion. Mules, Shetland ponies, pigs, beagles and all kinds of chickens: Bantams, Rhode Island Reds,Domineckers and an occasional exotic breed would fill our back and barn yard with entertainment rivaling Ringling Brothers. Purple Martins visited twice a year in elaborate three and four story houses he built from plans he'd ordered from *The Progressive Farmer.* He rigged the poles that held the bird hotels so we could lower them after they migrated to rid them of mites and their abandoned nests. He was a veterinarian without a framed certificate on the wall.

Daddy would take me to see baby calves being born. He told me the first time I saw this startling event while we were riding back home, I said to him, "Daddy, how fast was that baby calf going when it ran into its Mama?"

He told jokes as easy as breathing. Often at the expense of Mama. His favorite was when we visited relatives or friends. He would say, "Well, I had to bring Helen along so I wouldn't have to kiss her goodbye!" He reveled in fooling her on the first day of April. She either never caught on or humored him to keep him corralled for the rest of the year.

The two we remember went something like this. Mrs. Ella Etheridge had called him to tell my Mama she was ready to be taken to the Doctor for her check-up. Mama got ready to go, drove up to Mrs. Ella's house and honked the horn. Mrs. Ella came to the door and yelled, "Helen, what's all that honking about?" "Aren't you ready yet, Mrs. Ella?" my Mama said. "Ready for what, Helen?" Then it hit Mama too late; he had done it again.

Then there was the time Daddy had gotten up earlier than Mama, sneaked into the kitchen in the dark and yelled into the bedroom, "Helen get up, the pipes have burst and the kitchen is flooded!" He loved telling how Mama came tiptoeing into

179

The loggerhead turtle & my Daddy

the kitchen with her nightgown hiked up to her knees, and as he switched on the light, she stood there expecting her next step to be wading in water. He never told us what she said. He didn't curse.

The only down side to his tomfoolery was that Mama would simmer for days after being tricked. Come to think of it, that's probably why Daddy went to such elaborate planning. After one of his pranks, the house would be very quiet, and Mama wouldn't ask him to help her do anything inside or out.

But for 63 years their marriage more than just lasted. When Daddy and my sisters and I discussed what to put on Mama's tombstone, he asked very quietly if we could have "Married for 63 years" up near the top. And we did.

Daddy's existence was solely for us. And of course for others in need. He was a fine hunter who killed only for necessity. It was never about how many but about how much. How much would it take to top off the freezer in the utility room or how much the bag limit was. His integrity was sterling. Once he built me a live trap out of carefully cut one inch by one inch stakes that we fashioned into an open framed pyramid. He showed me how to rig it so one side was braced up with a stick that had bait tied to it up under the trap. If I caught a bird or baby rabbit the open sides would let it live until I could set it free. I would check it daily. Before I got to it one day I saw the bright red of a cardinal fluttering inside the sprung trap. I got so excited and wanted to show Daddy how smart he was so I managed to lift the trap, grab the exhausted red bird, and put him tightly in my coat. I squeezed it as I ran all the way home. He was in the kitchen when I yelled, "Daddy, look what we caught!" I opened my coat and one of the most beautiful things in nature fell from my coat to the floor. I had smothered it to death. He held me as I cried and simply said, "Son, you didn't intend to kill it." We buried it in an empty kitchen match box. I didn't have to ask him, but the next time I got the courage to go near the trap, it was gone.

Daddy's garden on the hill, about one hundred yards from the house, was as prize winning as any in the country. He planted after the last frost, usually around the middle of April, and the expected purple hull peas, okra, butter beans, squash, sweet corn and potatoes were planted in rows arrow straight and fenced off over the years with first wood then chicken wire, and finally an electric fence. Scarecrows were dressed in anything Daddy no longer wore, from flannel shirts to the last one I remember, his beige polyester leisure jacket. It never turned to shreds like the others. Polyester leisure suits have the half life of radio active fuel rods in nuclear plants.

Daddy's polyester scarecrow

There are two things I remember most vividly about my Daddy's garden. He always planted an entire row of Zinnias for my Mama to have flowers for the kitchen table or to take to church. That streak of reds, yellows, oranges, and pinks, on the row nearest the house, was a Crayola brush stroke underlining the many shades of green that fed us into the next spring.

The second vivid garden memory had nothing to do with color. I mentioned that my Daddy never cursed. Well, I don't remember him cursing... but once. I was following him and the plow mule planting some seeds in the new row when all of a sudden the mule stumbled, or as Daddy would tell me later, "He foundered," and then fell sideways into Daddy's perfect turnip patch, and began to kick and wallow and trash about trying to get back up. Tangled in the plow ropes and Daddy doing his best to upright the plow and not cut the mule created an ending scene of turnip destruction. There, in the usually silent garden air except for an occasional "Gee" or "Haw" or a mule snort, I heard my Daddy yell in the melee, "Goddammit, mule! Get out of my turnips!"

The mule got up immediately. My Daddy was so mad we all left the garden. On the way to the house without turning around, I heard him say, "Son, I'm sorry you had to hear that, but sometimes you have got to get a mule's attention."

In his last days at the house, before he had to be taken to the hospital and shortly thereafter died in the adjourning nursing home, I got to take care of Daddy in his own room. There was no conversation that amounted to very much, but we didn't have to talk. He was so weak it was a great effort for him just to sit up. I bathed him, and tried to get him to drink his Ensure, but we all knew that gentle night was coming. I slept in my parents' bed while he laid in the hospital bed near the windows. One night he woke me up trying to get over the rails to get to the little room in which he had installed his sink and mirror where he would clean up from a day's work. He was probably trying to get ready for the next day. I'm sure he had been lying there thinking about all the things that had to be done around the house.

Maybe he would start planning the garden soon. It was March, and next month was going to be a very busy time of his year.

My Daddy

9 789609 947046